COLLECTED POEMS

ISBN 978-1-952939-85-3 (hardcover set)
ISBN 978-1-952939-05-1 (hardcover volume I)
ISBN 978-1-952939-16-7 (hardcover volume II)
ISBN 978-1-952939-40-2 (paperback)

Library of Congress Control Number: 2020910346

ARIEL JASTROMB   COLLECTED POEMS

VOLUME I

A DECLARATION OF EXISTENCE

BLACKBIRD
ARTS PRESS

To all poets everywhere

TABLE OF CONTENTS

LATER POEMS

INTRODUCTION

"You were only waiting for this moment to arrive"

*A*RIEL CAME INTO THE WORLD hearing the John Lennon/ Paul McCartney song "Blackbird" and her life seemed to mimic the theme. She struggled with life's challenges and emerged free with words flowing out of her—finally "learning to fly."

Unbridled passion, deep-rooted empathy and raw sensitivity lay at the heart of Ariel's emotional being: at times it was woven with naiveté blinded by the needs of others and the dreams of what could be. On other occasions it was so complex, so filled with darkness and pain, that even the most learned were challenged to comprehend.

This depth of spirit and feeling was nurtured from an early age. While attending Ariel's third grade parent-teacher conference, her teacher pointed to two bins on the windowsill. The one on the left contained writings from all the students in the class, the other, overflowing, was dedicated to Ariel's work. We knew then she would be a writer.

Creativity permeated everything Ariel did. She had a unique sense of fashion, she explored the medium of music, mastering the piano, and she had a beautiful voice. Too, Ariel fell in love with the theatre. The art of acting served as an outlet for her to live vicariously through her characters.

Ariel attended Vassar College where her love of the written word flourished, honing her interest in poetry. The Hudson Valley had a great influence on her. With Halloween her favorite holiday, she spent hours applying makeup and perfecting her costume so as to transform her being. In particular, Sleepy Hollow and its legend lured her in, becoming a beacon of where she dreamed of living and a magical environ to spend her days writing. To this end, each year "The Legend of Sleepy Hollow" is read at the Old Dutch Church on October 31st in Ariel's memory.

While she grew up in the midwest, Ariel believed she was a true New Yorker and loved the city: its beauty, grit and all of its blemishes. She drew her inspiration from its streets, which tantalized her senses, and her words were influenced by its music, art, nature and culture. She published two chapbooks and started a literary magazine. Her writing was a visceral expression of her experiences and her vision of the world, its gifts and cruelties reflecting her most deep-rooted thoughts and feelings.

Beyond her compassion and sensitivity, Ariel was a fierce and loyal friend. She felt and loved deeply for the world to see. She was passionate and creative, determined to make her mark. She was good, drawn to those societal underdogs struggling to survive and be accepted.

Ariel accomplished so much in her all too short life.

These are her words we would like to share with you. We hope you see her for the beautiful, talented, sweet and complicated person she was.

—JOEL AND DIANE JASTROMB

○ ◑ ◕ ● ◕ ◐ ○

"It's not in the stars to hold our destiny, but in ourselves."
WILLIAM SHAKESPEARE

EARLY POEMS

AVANT GARDE

To be Modern is to master the mix—to make a bold
bright statement glitter
in the blacks and whites and grays.

I've swallowed a ruby, red as a hot spark shot-up
like a frantic firefly with pleasure.
It glows...my lipstick! Flick Flick
Flicking the tip of a cigarette

I repeat, *I am not!*
cast aside like a dull diamond
waiting for an empty setting.

I'm replete with killer heels and a silk shift dress,
the best!
Set ablaze in a Fashion Magazine.

Every night is heating up
The sky is full of pearls!
We're coming quick into a culture
fascinated with the distance,
fascinated by the ephemeral burst of imagination.

Shuffled like a stack of cards
split facedown,
we're anonymous, lonely.
We're dying to be dealt
but we're living to play
and playing to be heard.

SMART CONNECTION

Full-blown in silence and violent waves,
my back is turned but you'll knock me down.
There's an elephant on my chest,
compressed. There's an ache that reads
a joyful choke of the throat.

Oh...I'll break into a new city like a felon in the night—
silver glint of skyscraper
just scraping a sky
sick with stars and stellar debris.
A lovely man presses his palms to my thigh—
Dear God! I've done something right!

I'll witness bullets of rain
shooting pavement sixteen floors above.
The man of mine will study my face,
will study my body like a map and trace
places...
He'll weld the mess of metal bits you left
dangling, making me whole, I think.

But I'll always know you.
The love you send,
Unsolicited and silent.
I'll feel you,
face to floor,
smashed to pieces,
wondering when I'll see you next,
and wondering what you'll never say.

PAPARAZZI

I'm sitting at a bistro in Chelsea
where the dogs walk the men
and Intermezzo serves bellinis,
bloody marys and mimosas
Sunday, for free.

The lady in the broad-brimmed hat
tips a cigarette, fire first,
haphazard into a high-ball
clotted with ice.
Her eyes, they're peridots sinking
under the gems on her hat — big, heavy-lidded
almost clumsy.
She leaves the check with a Chippendale.
Her posture — rigid, packed tight and faltering slightly,
trapped in stiletto pumps.

A man with a camera snaps quickly away,
just enough to catch an awkward flash
of chiseled abs and something in her pants!

She's got a show on the Bowery
where the lights are low
yet pointed on her sequined dress.
Fans from here and there and Europe
clamor for a serenade.

So this is flash,
this is glam,
this is where Bobby goes,

searching for someone to absorb the affection he's set
adrift, floating down the street, cross-town
and huddled in a bar.

1965 BRIGITTE BARDOT

Black lined cat eye bleeds
watercolor-like, a living work of art
huddled in a dead animal zoo.
Sweet dazzling lips smack brightly —
strange — because it's so dark
Yet I can still see!

ALL MOD CONS

What's that there in that threadbare
pocket in your second-hand plaid?
Only the best cigarettes from the finest
most UNDERGROUND shop in New York or L.A.
So Underground you had to dig for days
through the gritty earth —
you've forgotten where you've stayed.

Club kid extraordinaire,
imagine the taste,
the shape of life when you're old.
What'll you write?
Who will know where you spend your days?

In that second-hand shirt they won't see you!
They'll see
Mr. Working Class Stiff,
hell-bent on success,
tending a farm somewhere in Illinois, 1965.
"Praise the beauty of simplicity—of honest work that 'NOWADAYS'
no one understands, that NOWADAYS seems so rare."

It'll be like you never existed

MUSIC IS MY RELIGION

When little girls dressed in white
and boys with slicked-down hair
tag-along behind rumpled parents to church
I wonder, sometimes, if maybe I'd like to tag along too.

I'll pass the synagogue by my house in Chicago
noting small herds of bleary-eyed observers
cooing to their babies, fastening kippahs
and for a second, I think I'm jealous.

I'm pretty sure the inspiration comes from inside
as an outpouring of faith and devotion
as an outlet for fear and uncertainty.
Something that sounds like a beat of the heart
in someone else's hand.

I like to travel with my music, pounding pavement
to the Motor City Bar in New York
or down Fullerton to Mickey's and Jason's
maybe see Jude...hit the Mutiny for Old Style on tap.
They have an excellent jukebox—Joan Jett, The Stooges,
The Rolling Stones! Gimme Shelter, as they sing.

The place couldn't be dirtier.
The pews are barstools and bar-flys, the parishioners.
The bartenders are saints for putting up with confessional trash
but the beat's all I need.

I'm not sure about heaven or hell, but I'm sure as hell here
with too much makeup,

too much jewelry
and a penchant for bleeding my heart into the like of Joan, Iggy,
     and Mick and the Boys.

L'AMERICAINE SNOB

Have you seen the fall collections?
Can you believe Elbaz for Lanvin? I know—
his work really caught the upswing, just gets better and better—
don't you think?
And what about Gucci...I'm still missing Tom Ford. I know—
his eyewear and perfume collections are doing quite well
but aren't you just dying for a reason to show some skin without
        feeling like an utter
casualty like Paris Hilton or some godawful nocialite?
And haven't you seen that girl....you know, the one with the terrible
        highlights
and terrible nose-job to boot?
APPARENTLY—she's going to rehab.
I KNOW!

I mean, she had it coming.
Her husband's leaving her for his Chinese mistress...
Some people have no class.
I heard she offered the immigration officer
sexual favors!
Can you believe it?
I mean, how desperate?

Before I head to Nora's, you know the Gala is tomorrow night.
Yes, I'm wearing Balenciaga. Just brilliant.
And You?
Shut Up! Oliver Theyskens! But isn't that risky?
He just took the post at Nina Ricci! I know.... Reese Witherspoon
        already...
I guess that's legitimate.

At least *she* won't be there.

You heard, didn't you? You do remember the MOMA debacle?

Ugh, she's a head on a stick.

I would be too if I siphoned thirty Percocets a day.

Must be that awful mother-in-law of hers.

Some people are so unfortunate.

STOP MAKING SENSE!

You and I are listening—closely—to the Talking Heads,
sharing a fifth of gin,
cozy with the familiar fear of hands touching
electric to one another.

John Ashbery says New York owns travelers shifting
from one life into another,
transitory, spaceless and shapeless.

I'm from Chicago, where city meets soul
and you're an island of blue and gray.
I'm Schiele and you are Basquiat
with a passport to Austria, but
we're pattern recognition, as Kim Gordon sang.

It all fits, all's in place.
We're both foreigners in Gotham
like tidy characters bound to a plot.
It's perfect—we're perfect without blinders,
tête-a-tête, head to head.

I'm struggling for an ending but
it'll just be a smokescreen protected from lightness,
from nature, or "naturalness" but
I'm dizzy with your strokes
fresh-faced, alive but ailing
an undernourished heart.

OCTOBER

When my mind,
like a sack of pearls
tumbles and repeats,
I trust that I am manifold —
shaded and deeply marked
as a bold Tahitian.

I am open with the sea—rough pit
of many organisms—
grains that soften, polish
and cast me out.
I glow, irregular with the moon.

When I lay in your bed
asleep, but feeling,
your arms like shells clamped-shut
rock me
with the tearing of expected waves.

It is night and we are milling the rubble in thick
pools of me.
My hand is sweating safely in your palm
and I imagine tomorrow as
gray light creeping across my face,
brilliant and new.

FOR GERTI

On viewing Egon Schiele's "Semi-Nude Girl, Reclining, 1911"

Every light begins a coma.
The black ink of darkness
crawls across the room like spiders
scattered in their webs.
Onyx and silk,
they are the glitter of the night.

I am asleep and listening to every word.
My skeleton rests heavy with inklings,
bone-flints of dark purpose.
My blood is electric in my veins,
metallic as a beetle's shell.

In the death of night
I am precious as a jewel
His brush, moist on a troubled canvas,
screams in feverish strokes—
brutal lines sick with rough color.

I hear we're most receptive in our sleep
but I will not dream.
I see Vienna in December,
slicked with ice and steely as the sky.
I see the death of things
once alive and hidden, revealed.

WHAT MAY NEVER BE

Few can touch this Dead, cold grave
What stones are these to try and save?
They mock me in this wintry haze
Shifting with the Lunar phase.

Try as might we wish to spare
A glistening lock of Venus hair
When Cycles freeze abrupt; unclear
This silent stillness holds my fear.

Bitter pills to swallow fast
Can Barren soil truly last?
What Ghost is this for me to hold?
No future here for her to mold.

This stretch of land screams out for one
To grace it with the Healing sun
Who cares if shadows comfort me when
Shadows are all they'll ever be.

NERVOUS SPLENDOR

Here, we are nearly burlesque,
all exaggerated curves and neon absurdity,
electric fictions in a carnival of anxiety.
Dark-mouthed, we group like moths,
boxed hearts rattling, fixed eyes
warm to the narcotic light.

I'm not interested in this rough-hewn
network of truths, I said, this fabric of infallibility.
I'm interested in the gaps—things that were, collapsed,
connected only by their absence.

Tonight the pulse of midnight desperation
chokes the room with waves of sickened oxygen,
exposed nerves deaf to familiar voids.
My lips are lacquered cherries,
vinyl buds I painted,
pained to exist beyond themselves.

I wonder what they look like outside,
if they project as fierce a red
when you and I make faces in the dark.

NIGHT AND DAY IN THE DESERT

Night in the desert is different than day,

For us it would be strange to live the desert way.

It is cool and the sky sparkles with beautiful colors in the night,

In the day it shows off its startling rays of amazing light.

The animals find a way to survive and bear the desert heat,

But at night when the desert cools the sun is beat.

So this is where the animals roam,

To them the desert is home.

Day or Night.

2009

46 DAYS CLEAN

Two men in conversation on a sunny day—
it's L.A. – far from these guitars, in pain.
They weep in New York City.

46 days, I've done my counting,
in and out of craggy spaces,
murky places—faceless, nameless—
hated all the same.

And yet, today's a fight
monstrous unlike the others
slides under the skin slug-like
and rubs the heads of pins.

The twinge of raw nerve
coursing through mind and body,
bulging eyes, chatter of teeth
46 days and clean

ESCAPE FROM THE CITY

We left a sea of heads bathed in neon,
electric in the dark.
The spark of fireflies undone, we slipped like cherries,
lazy, silk-like and tumbling
through the genteel drawl, the warm thickness
of a rye Manhattan.
We are numb below the surface.

We left them, cut out our eyes, and ate them.
When we couldn't see we could taste
metallic, all that we had missed.

In the blindness we were magnetic—
I to you, you to me.
You lingered in the blood, a flood on my cheek;
I tasted yours to know how it felt to cry.

Your fingertips, tapping lightly,
trace my spine—
A map of where we'll go from here.
Your heart, a furious creature,
beats and we are underground where,
for once, we are alone and terribly alive.

SPRING IN CONNECTICUT

The stench of city platforms and garbage
rotted by the sun isn't here where everything is clear,
bright, opiate, nameless, opaque.

Give me the dimmest bar on a stretch of blackened city block
slick with rain, bold and achingly charged—
silver cobbled slivers of moon.

The cityscape is challenged beauty;
it gleams in gritty bits that stick in my throat.
This spring time air in Connecticut can choke,
maim, destroy, revive...

It's easy to hide this sickness in the shade
where trees spit pollen like satellites,
wind uninhibited, a swift carrier.
Brightness of city nights,
shuttered stores, noise and fights,
anonymity you may believe.

Keep quiet, keep still.
the city has eyes.

THE MOORS IN NEW ENGLAND

I shouldn't call them 'moors' because they are not,
yet come cold spring meadows and valleys,
cloaked in fog thick and wild, resemble English moors.
Color of heather, texture of peat. The haze of Haldol.

Evening comes whisper-like along a neurotic river,
shallow and jagged with rocks.
The house, perched grimly over a sickly pond,
sighs horrible secrets and guards
country club china that no one sees.

This nightmare...rustlings in the leaves of moaning trees,
ghostlings collapsed in every weathered flower...
and the geese...the roving geese!

The maddening moors of New England take from you,
when you drift, when you shift attention
from the phantom mallards that wade among the dead
through the wet, bracing wind through which
you cannot, will not and should not ever see.

HOMECOMING

The wild country roads of dandelion weeds
Are tamed by belts of city air blown from the South.
Where everything is civil and laid like square-pegged tiles.
The old buildings, mausoleums of the rich, are tattered lace;
Gray faded patterns spread like a lattice on the face of an angel.
This Uptown, narcotic place in NouveauYork
in a decrepit family relic,
Whose coffins are only shells left sinking
In an ancient sea,
I think I'd like to be married
In tattered silk the color of ivory
Set ablaze with matches – how I love that "new match" smell.
I'll carry a bunch of lilies and branches from the Park
Where the trees still happen to flower
Despite the weather.
Should we buy a home
In the canyons of the creatures of the past
And call it "pre-war?"
Oh, the dead!
How I wish them all as colorful as Peggy Guggenheim—
The world is not so serious!
If we take it as such,
We are sure to burn another one out.

ON COCAINE

I live like a movie star and always have.
Every day's a show, every night's party
and I *sparkle*.

The buzzing numb of cocaine and I'm tearing through the room.
Dresses, heels, lashes, bangles,
earrings as big as my face.
Scotch and coke, coke and Scotch,
All kindling for the hostess—
I play with fire.

Never have I looked so glamorous,
never have I felt so famous,
talking to my cat, traipsing 'round the room,
searching for cameras hidden in the walls.

It's getting late, I'm almost on,
my guests arrive in bloom!
I shimmer, shock and soothe—
a fairy dragged through dust so thick
I'm the only one who knows
I glow.

My face, the cover of a magazine
that none of us has ever seen.

FOR LARS ON HIS BIRTHDAY

Dearest Lars, your life begins today.
Brutal slice of morning shot through curtains drawn,
fistfuls of tears, all diamonds, thrown like knives to the wall.

The cloying darkness that surrounds you, drowns you,
now drains.
The pattern of your breath is fluid in your lungs—
a respite, small joy though it is.

Your angel hair and haunted eyes—
what a gift, what a treasure we have found!
You haven't the sound to shriek or cry
so you struggle in your skin,
gracefully broken, perfect as a plotted photograph.

Put your hand in mine and feel its pulse
pumping blood, daring yours to do the same.
Skim this tender ribbon scar of mine,
know that I have been there too.

A picture's only touching if it moves you;
A man is only happy if he tries.

KILLING TIME

The seats were wet with migrant snow.
You, me, a bowl of cold Pad Thai,
one soggy tabloid and three painted hookers
aboard a train to the West Village.

Our fingers traced the subway map.

Exit to Eden of iron gates,
I collapsed into the strength of your arms.
Against a mural, blaze of city wall,
we kissed—intimate and public.

A breath together and we broke,
staggered by the pulsing of our hearts.

DEMONS

Begin syrup-like in my spine.
Vertebra after vertebra they creep and hit skull.
Inklings in the corner of my eye,
shadows slumped in corners—
a fly, mosquito, cicada—
demons are shape-shifters.

They live in the mirrors and behind the eyes—
flecks of gold dust married by dead aggression.
They prey on the brain and drain blood to pass the time.
They observe, deceive, taunt the body that now
stands hollow, make-believe tree.

I live with their curious tricks and ploys
continuously,
a record on the turntable.
Stuff and steal, stuff and steal,
I am filled with bricks
standing, waiting, fearing the tingle at the base of my neck.

The trouble permeates in waves,
I am naked unto myself.

ATYPICAL LOVE LETTER

She sits in a Swedish chair
ten floors high
peeling grapes like eyes.
Popping them—one, two, three—
her mouth plump, her cheeks full.
Across the street a neon 'cocktail' sign
flickers in an empty bar.

She's all alone and peeling grapes.
sucking eyes that once were his.
A stricken cigarette.
Smoke purrs kitten-like, curling,
a coiling fluff of calm,
'...my lover...' she drones.

Now fistfuls of eyes—pop, pop—
sparse apartment haunted by his space.
dishes built up. Little towers in the sink.
'Where have you gone?'

Pop, pop. squeeze...
the zombie moans become banshee cries.
Pulp oozes through a raw, bitten grasp.
She's full of eyes, there are no more.
In hopes that he will see the beast that has become her pain.

THIS MAN

By my side is more than a boy grown tall.
Sometimes he wears a suit
underneath which something unescapable shows,
reaching tentacles into my own,
hearts beating like boxes
clamoring electric, clamped shut like shells.

Wild trail tamed in a sense,
me and him, Scotch and gin.
The ebb and flow of ocean time,
barnacles, tide pools, slugs—
sometime when the water's calm
find me happy, buried in the sand and smiling—
I'm yours and that is all.

SOBER ACTIVITY SMOKING CIGARS

We're slouched like strangers in paradise
in grandfather chairs, a room all alone.
We smoke cigars
because it's something to do.

Limbs fizzy, buzzing mind
I sketch your portrait with mahogany words—
your crinkle eyes a well-worn book.

Tonight we are adults
playing dress-up with our feelings.
We sate our hungry hearts with careful conversation
I feel I'll always be waiting for you.

Smoke billows languidly,
this banging in my chest,
I'm grateful for this moment,
a requiem for childhood.

The familiar sound of your soul stepping lightly
clutching fearlessly to mine.

BURNHAM BEACH

Sick little stars speckle the Chicago skyline.
The blaze of city night eats my view.
Freshwater seashells and velvety rock skeletons
gravitate towards yesterday's trash—
Unimportants shimmering under faint moonlight.

I can smell the gas from Lake Shore Drive—
a kind of perfume almost sentimental when
pooled with the smelly fish lake.

"Sit on the pier," he says.
I do.
My face burns fierce and I see
all things dead, alive and twinkling.

THE FIRESIDE BOWL

Acid greens and blues drip aloof—
The graffiti on the walls pregnant
with freshness. That neon flamingo
in the bar across the street pulses—
quiet, steady.

Like a Jim Jarmusch film we are gray
present in nothing but this moment.
All of us, a mob of motley souls
bob our heads to the electric lilt
of synthetic sonatas
into cigarette air.

It is at the Fireside Bowl
Where kids like us find our
rocking
rolling
solidarity.

VENUS FLY-TRAP

Here a perfect creature sits
Carnivorous and salty-sweet.
Cherry-blossom lips ache to be plucked.
Frosty breasts peek from under her vines.

Tell me, dear Roman goddess,
All you do is scintillate.
I break you with my teeth
And fry your leaves for breakfast.

Green glitter pours from your eyes
My hands dirty with emeralds.
I shriek into your face
You swallow my tongue whole.

LEARNING TO SKATE #1

Head tweaked to the side, your hair looks funny today.
I think you meant to comb your curls
        and change your shirt
yet somehow
I KNOW you didn't.

Spitting gum under the bridge
It sighs beneath our feet.
        You say
today's the day
I HAVE to learn to skateboard.

THE STRIPPER

Body full of sparks
Marissa jolts to the motion of
sweaty palms rubbing the dark.

She smiles silly,
fondling her gun at
a colony of urban hillbillies.

Naked, she'd shoot us all
but Rico buys diapers for Baby.
John supplies her phenobarbital.

She swivels and crucifies
aggressive Washingtons,
stilettos nearly grazing her thighs.

I thought I saw her move the earth with her scream
but Daniel's been drinking out of a bag.
He's living the seamless American dream.

She peels in strips—the stripper
b l e e d s.
We've whipped her.

I want to catch a piece of her,
my wallet bulky with movie stubs
and change is where I'll keep her.

I'd like to wear her party dress
and drop it to the stage.
If she had it her way, we'd be lifeless
Split somewhere in sick.

She'd rob us clean.

THE "JELLYFISH"

The Man-of-War is a curious monstrosity.
I met the creature on a Florida key,
quite near the top of the sun.
Jelly-filled and bulging,
the sack was a bauble in a sea of pearls.
It bullied waves as commander of ship and burst,
an aquatic *aurora borealis*,
over the swimming citizens of its shadow.
Absorbing amber rays through an ample pouch,
its purplish legs and arms
dappled the liquid surface of a shallow sandbar.
I, far from shore, awaited its arrival
and watched the big lump waddle to my finger,
stretched to greet the glorious beast.
Arms spread in spasm, it met my touch
with a shock so electric,
my arm pulsed with jelly buttons.
I *would* have cried at the injustice,
yet in the tide of excitement I exacted my revenge.
From my swollen grasp
dangled, unknowing,
half an arm, lopped clear from that fish!

RECITING THE CLASSICS

Flicking cigarettes into an empty street
We grace the stoops—all pigeon-poop-
Slathered, sticky and spread on the seat of my jeans.
We are the youngest of the youth.

Off to loftier places to dump our trash,
We sift through years of molten things.
Aglow, they burn salty as asphalt grit—
A swift cracking of square-pegged teeth.

PHYSICAL LOVE

When she was young she wandered the water,
collecting shells and coral and everyday
dead jellyfish strewn as wasted things across the sand.
After the collection of small beings,
(some starfish, sand dollars), little creatures that used to breathe
saturated her wicker basket in silent struggle.
Lifeless for hours, they lay in heaps of sea-bodies,
dry, pale, and less lonely than before she scooped them up
in her creaky house of lost water souls.
She set the table (a starved tree-stump by the gate),
and laid her victims—sticky jellys, round and floppy,
on a rougher surface than that of the sea.
Cutting through the soft gelatin of organism,
she pieced away bits of animal precisely
with shards of dulling sea-glass—instruments gleaming
in the dull beam of early morning sun.
The enigma of jelly-fish blood—clear silk
spilled over the discs. She messed her dress and screamed,
willing the tiny legless beasts to rumple with breath.
Liquid and elegant, they died a second instant
at the hands of someone who loved them as children
and cared enough to kill them with her tiny bare hands.

COMPASSION FOR THE ENEMY

A lotus blossom sticks down roots
if only as a gesture.

The pink folds into itself.
Petals gape and close.

A symbol in stasis,
wound in water,

the lotus blossom breathes
and throbs and shuts itself.

The moon, in color,
swallows up the dark.

THE PYGMY HIPPO

I've come to see the shy river horse
who monopolized my youngest affections.
Before growth and production, his silk-slicked skin
shone—the arbiter of innate delight—
as a gleaming heap of amethyst
couched in the mud of earthly leisure.

His ears are round little oars.
They propel him nose first, through inlets of holy murk.
A silent giant dwarfed, he squeals, vocal—
alone in his filth at last!

The cameras have left yet I remain
his tireless devotee.
I fish wrist and forearm, inmates
through the metal barrier, and reach...

If I were tall we could stew together,
friends in a world constructed by caretakers.
We'd banter noiseless through the thick of our artificial canal—
the flash of visitors deaf to our plotting.

THE BUSINESS OF BEING PERSONAL

I am a rag doll, naked in mesh.
I own a belly, pointed breasts,
awkward shuffle of jet heels.
You and I are rigid—rusted
save for your cigarette smoke.

Your hands are clams,
moist and clamped shut
on my pillow hips.
We sway robotic. Metal
only *tastes* like blood.

We are counterfeit to one another.
All the lights are naked, too.
Dusty girls—spiders in the corner—
practice lies
and cross their ample thighs.

KULTUR NEWS

I never read the paper
but today I decide to pose as a real
working functional person in a real
broken dysfunctional city.

I read in "Sunday Styles"
we're contracting something called
"Cosmopolitanism."
Apparently China's caught up,
Germany's rebuilt,
India's bursting at the seams
and America's got something like dysentery.

New York's rent inflation's creating
pools of populations,
of hipsters, of yuppies, of everyday
robots, superheroes and apathetic worms
pulling for Brooklyn, fleeing to Astoria and
Europe's got the flu.

Perhaps I'll go to Shanghai—
apartment with a view,
shiny and new, bending to the river.

I'll shop in what looks like SoHo
and drink with all the expat Germans
nestled in Face, or another booming bar
blooming in the French quarter.

"China's the new Brooklyn,"
Brooklyn's the new China
and either way we'll still be looking
for a place with lower rents,
classy "ethnic" restaurants,
big-money townhouses
and loads of street credibility.

1971 BIANCA E MICK JAGGER

"What kind of man are you?"
she beams from across the room.
Slow, steady crackling of knuckles—his
eyes like a scanner,
her slick leopard lick of ice cream or gelato.

"I am a small school of fish," he laughs,
breath pulled through like a dandelion
bursting through the street at the corner of Ludlow & Rivington.
Mellow alien, vibrant and skeletal—
he's unbearably magnificent.

"We're lovers, you and I," she says,
"electric, fraught with charge—
we're magnets like the stars."

But Oh!
Fluorescent goldmine of lies
built in love, laid like tiles—
a mosaic of what happens when fire meets
the captor of its flame.

They spilled their drinks on the gondola
carried away like two kids
nestled in the comfort of Venice, sinking.

MIDWEST TRANSPLANT

I was born in Chicago, grew up in Chicago, had my first drink in
    Chicago, lost my virginity in
Chicago, met the most wonderful people in Chicago.
Damaged people full of light
skeletons all, in pilfered tombs
where one might lay their head.
I know...I feel...
In Chicago
winter is cruel, merciless,
wind-whipped, frozen and long;
It starts in December, maybe November
when I stood outside The Fireside Bowl
Seven dollars for a ticket for five bands
playing electric in the dark. And I smoked cigarettes,
smoked a pack in one go
because I was there
because I could,
because I wanted to see
Debbie Harry and Blondie,
The Ramones, Television and Patti Smith.
If I were in New York in 1974...
I wasn't.
I was Midwestern girl, looking to New York for the life of a star.
New York hasn't Lake Michigan
Chicago, no Bowery.
It's give and give and give and sometimes take it if you can
No matter where you go.

WORLD TRADE CENTER SPECTERS

The hole in the ground, now seven years old, is still a hole.
Lower Manhattan is no town, still, because it is full of ghosts.
The Downtown Alliance built living spaces
like mine
in the skeletons of office buildings where men and women
jumped to their deaths.

Others perished, rats trapped in stairwells
when the buildings rattled, splintered and fell.
The proudest few, I imagine,
spilled slow-motion tears in glasses of brandy
soggy cigar in mouth, to watch the show.
The skyline crashed and spewed forth flames—the color of which,
in another context,
might have been beautiful.

The façade of my building, charcoal-black.
Smoke smolders still, after seven years.
In the lobby everything is shiny white marble.
Enormous lion-shaped fountains roar
behind bars, a proliferation of useless columns,
as if to suggest a visit to a Florentine piazza
and not a relic of Wall Street prowess.

My building is the end of the world.
It is built from bones, broken and jagged,
naked and silent as the mouth of hell.

The hallways are dangerous—they are not mine, nor yours.
An electric wonderland of lights dwindle

at night when elevators stall in their shafts.
It's freezing all of the time.

It's lonely every day—
A paralysis of the common condition where shadows
moan about this castle of bones
searching for their own in the hours of sleep.

But I am awake. I hear the drone of the dead
leafing through my bookshelf, resting on my sofa,
Watching television, like they used to
before the world around them died.
With mouths full of ashes,
they choked on horrible animal sounds
and the fight that never had a chance began and ended
in minutes
and they never screamed because they hadn't the time.

SEASONS IN MANHATTAN: WINTER

An island
Surrounded by water
Polluted with dreams and debris
Leaking from Fresh Kills—our trash a range of mountains.

It rains in winter, it snows sometimes
When wet flakes pumped-up, the size of a fist
Blanket the streets if only for a moment.
Roof-top gardens of bonsai, palms and flowers potted neatly
Strain in the wind—are maimed by it—
Lifeless sprouts of city love yearn for country hope.

Grey skies and a promise of rain, a wish for clean snow that,
    once fallen,
Becomes tarnished by
gritty streets and men in galoshes,
By yellow frosted taxi cabs stewing in the slush we call
Snow in Manhattan.

Christmas trees are plucked from any corner and lean in windows,
Stacked one on top of the other in apartment buildings—
Holiday spirit for those without windows—those without walls, too.

What a misery it must be to huddle in the bleakness of the season
Under tunnels,
On park benches
Watching those windows, wondering where *their* tree leans.

The city is dark much of the time.
Perhaps there is a less to see or maybe, more to feel.

Stark-blind in a shared sort of kindness
They fumble, together,
Fervent for a light.

SEASONS IN MANHATTAN: AUTUMN

Come Autumn each year,
The Hudson Valley blooms with the decadence of decay.

The trees are splendid in their sickness;
They have hands that ruffle fluidly like feathers,
Hands that spin green dark to die in beauty.
Then yellow then gold then orange then persimmon then plum.
Then brown.

Dirt claims what it cannot reach; those hands
Coddled by lawns bloody with bodies like their own.
Incapacitated and furious with rage,
Leaves shrivel and flake-apart
To be dragged into mudrooms by children with runny noses,
To be cast-out by an old man, sweating and cursing, with a rusty
rake.

The "turning" in Manhattan is sharp, jagged, miscalculated.

City-whipped leaves surrender to a sort of arrested development.
Some crumble to their deaths before summer departs.
Others, still green, cleave like bats to stable branches.

Many leaves disappear unnoticed, made invisible by
        street-sweepers,
Incessant traffic or muted, sulky rains that suck them into gutter
grates.
We didn't know because we couldn't see.

We had no evidence of struggle—no record at all.
We never saw it coming.
Anonymous Manhattan leaves,
Nameless Manhattan trees,
Ambitious yet restrained—
The buzzing hum of white noise
Lulling us to sleep.

PART-TIME LOVER

Clock-watcher:
When we're on, we're fatal,
You and I gasping in my ear.
And then we're off until we can't forget.
Collapsing into one another,

A silent rage screaming loud,
The shudder of tears shed—
Inept, anti-recovery and thick—
You are the cruelest drug that I can't kick.

I'm sick of sleeping with shadows
Electric and mute.
I love you sometimes,
I think of you always,
And in this mess I'm true
And you are straight with no one.

If you could see these monsters
I would stop my life to care.
But kisses and their breathy words are only whispers.
It's quiet here.

Catch me,
Feel me,
Show me something that doesn't kill,
Something that's real.
Show me how to feel.

Only in the dark, I see nothing but you,
Light is everything that you can't be.

Though you are sicker than I,
It will always be me,
the one that bleeds.

THIS IS NOT MY CITY

This sleepless City collapses
Continuously,
Crumbles and folds
Continuously,
Into itself.

This is a city of sketches,
Of gestures, traces, inklings—
All ghosts.

I see

Flickering in my eye,
Shapeless shadow figures slumped in subway cars like sacks of pota-
toes.

They linger...
Blurry blots and blips half-formed,
Thwarted, abject cries declaring desperately
I was here! We were here!

These little pictures projected are glue,
A stagnant, spun-cotton haze of history that glazes the City.
They are the difference between leveling and layering,
Between faking and feeling.

I feel deeply.

Honest and odd of mind, I see those specs that shimmer sadly—
Gloomy sparkles scattered on these pages,
Settled, present, here.

WELCOME BACK (2-MINUTE POEM)

Yesterday I met a junkie
Cooking up on Rivington
Where he stared for hours at nothing
Before New York was clean.
And now we feel the quake—the city's crashing,
I should think.

He's back on stoop with spoon, alone
To roam the streets he's learned by force.
Pure, pure democracy,
Shopping carts as far as I can see.

Whatever happened to New York City?
Priced-out, we'd never know.
But when the dead are out and begging for quarters,
Dogs and cats in sweaters singing.
I haven't a dime and neither does anyone I know.

I know a place where kids get clean
Confess their sins and show their bones.
Blazing, ancient old-time lovers,
New York,
We call it home.

NIGHT JOURNEY

I.

A cautious moon propped itself up in the sky
Splitting silver shards of glass into the lake.
Fishing for pearls in a freshwater bowl of soup,
Kitty scraped the sand with her giant spoon.
The boat, wooden cracking back and forth,
Split in two, wetting Kitty's eyes and
Sinking...
To the bottom of the lake.
Fists full of shellfish, barnacles on her shins,
Kitty surfaces, sliding to the center of her shiny spoon.

II.

Tedium makes it harder to float when the Salt
In the water has left for the ocean.
Kitty, collecting oysters for pearls,
Asks the moon to shine brighter so that
The pearls won't be lonely, glimmering in the dark.
The moon drifts lazily to the boat,
Sitting next to the oysters, glowing their shells.

III.

Prying open the first oyster, Kitty
Squirts...
Lemon juice and Tabasco onto the meat,
Slurping it quickly through her square teeth.
Chuckling happily with every discovery,
That each pearl shines, sparkling, more brilliant than
The one before
Reflecting the faint giggling of the moon.

HALLIE'S BABY

Where's Hallie McAdoo—
Teen check-out queen?
She used to shoot billiards in Golden Day Hall
And race little boys to Mr. Good Humor's truck.

Hair spit-blonde and sassy,
Eyes perpetually glassy,
Ms. McAdoo kicks up her Converse heels
And sprints gracefully clumsy and unaware.

I saw her the other day
Licking popsicle sticks in the back of the Church
Father Perish dovening inside her,
And she grew big with the tick of the clock.

Ready for Baby—a baby herself
Breathing in a safe place of
Cotton candy and hopscotch.
Hallie McAdoo hits the register to break a bill.

"Father, forgive me…"
A crippling breath fails in her throat.
As she bags my orange juice, cotton balls and napkins,
A gritty sharpened cry wretches itself from her lungs.

Dropping on her round belly,
Face-down in linoleum.

But she's on her feet again.
Hallie McAdoo just laughs and
Strolls
Merrily on her way.

SEQUINS

A ray of dirty yellow light
Flickering amidst these odd dots...
Building a fortress on my wall
In code, rainbow and shellacked
Across my bed frame.

A gallery of chipped finger-painted
Lady-killers parading around my
Eyelashes, Flashing their revolvers
From out under their vests
Cocking them to their throats.

A blast of magnet fire
Showering the room in gold...
Blood shimmering from the pores
In the wall like mesh,
A liquid smile bursting through my lips.

CHANNELING OSAKA

Pacific silk and brazen ladies
Politely shuffle their feet along the garden bridge.

Tight binding of obi sash
Crushing bamboo and hyacinth.

The watery flow of lilypad laughter
Escapes their painted mouths and pallid cheeks.

Bless this sake-drunken body,
Pull me under your many robes—

Layer upon layer of buttery film—
I can't seem to grasp them!

Teach me how to step as you do.
Cinch me into serpent ribbons,

And kiss me

So that I might grow to hold my tongue
Like You, comfortably lounging in my cheek.

LEARNING TO SKATE 2

Head tweaked to the side, your hair looks silly today.
I think you meant to comb your curls
And change your shirt
Yet somehow I know you didn't.

Spitting hum under the bridge
As it sighs beneath our feet
You say today's the day
I have to learn to skateboard.

Rough and sandy, your paws dug at my hips
Guiding the board away from the curb, but
Bump, bump, bbbump...
"It's okay," you laughed with your heart.

We've gone separate ways by now,
Traveling, working, growing up...
I know you're doing something wonderful
Because I've never met a more honest man.

No matter where I go
No matter whom I meet
I will always look back at
My first skateboarding lesson.

BUCKTOWN

Charged wind machetes the Chicago low-rises
As I grip weathered concrete with the
Sole
Of my feet...clip clip drip...
Quaint and crisp, the blurring of
Midwestern charm and urban decay
Nesting in the pit of my brain.
Playground of the forward-thinkers
And independent Nothing yuppies.
The French bakery invades my nostrils
I sit on the corner of Damen and Milwaukee
A bench where Gloria waits every hour
For a bus that will never arrive.
She asks me for a nickel to phone her son—
"He's a lawyer you know!"
Thick Polish corrupting her speech.
Marbled tears and muddled sighs,
Gloria wails!
What a sound!
Slinking away from the corner
I toss her two grimy quarters.
"The phones are fifty cents nowadays."
I break away,
Wild breeze whipping steadily
Keeping me afoot
Pressing Gloria to the bench.
The bus careens from around the street sign
To take her away.
A glance, and she fades.

PILLOW TALK

I wrestle with you in my bed of feathers
Pulling at your insides in my feather bed.
The blood in your eyes makes it difficult to see
Where you stab your knife, tickling my thigh.

I'd like to think we'll mellow with age
My hands fist-deep in your teeth,
But you will want to swallow me whole—
Head fists, knee, toe...

On my wall I've hung your dripping lungs—
They beat furiously despite the pins
I've stuck them with to keep you Home
And in my bed beside my brain.

Cauterize my bleating throat,
Collect my bones for flint,
Black my eyes until I chuckle
At the sight of feathers floating out my nostrils.

FOR YOU

His eyes shake me something steely blue
Burning, burrowing, boring icy dots in my head.
A mojito smile, the lick of sugar fluttering between his lips
I catch his breath, withering under the cigarette fog
Trailing from his tongue—up my spine in clicks
He whispers—I can't make out what you're saying!
A trip to the ocean, our blood, flotsam on the waves.
He dresses me in jewels, Diamonds!
Look how they sink my bones, mere flint and splintered
Bones. As they creep among the rippling blue
The same blue as your eyes—frozen yet moving.
I want to suffocate myself with his hands
As clear as my veins
As soft as his kiss
Breathe Me.

LAKE MICHIGAN

Climb me up your sandy dunes
As we make a picnic in your arms.
The ebb and flow of your freshwater giggles
Tickles my toes as I gaze at your view.

What used to be bottles from sottish bonfires
Washed foamy to your shore,
And we collect your precious sea jewels
For odds and ends and everyday nothings.

An enigmatic ingenue, though terrifyingly wise,
You scoop us into your frothy waters
Bending us every which way
Until we scream with joy, water streaming out our noses.

We hunt in the safety of your catch
And unlike the ocean, you'll never let us drift too far.
Cajoling us with seaweed and rocks
We clomp aimlessly into your trenches.

Never have we trusted anything but you,
The true blue glossy glint in your eye.
We give our souls to your monster touch
And pull ourselves forever under.

VENUS

There, sits this perfect creature
Carnivorous and salty-sweet.
Her cherry blossom-lips that ache to be plucked
And frosty breasts peeking out from under her vines.

Green glitter pours from her eyes
Dirtying my hands with Emeralds
As I shriek into her face
And swallow her tongue whole.

Teach me, dear Roman Goddess,
All you do is scintillate.
I want to break you with my teeth
And fry your leaves for breakfast.

AN EARLY MEMORY

I imagined my mother's clothes and lipsticks as elegance—
woven or packaged in little tubes.
I wore her whitest dress.
Pop Rocks spilled the corners of my mouth and settled,
as candy emblems of reminder—
little medals where my breasts would have been.
I wished I were thirty.
I strung my fakest jewels around my mother's neck,
the neck of a woman with rhinestones for eyes.
The things she saw, the truth she knew,
makes me wish I had listened.
Real women eat pizza in the morning when eggs are hard to come by.
Mirrors, indicators of imitation, seem clearer in the evening.

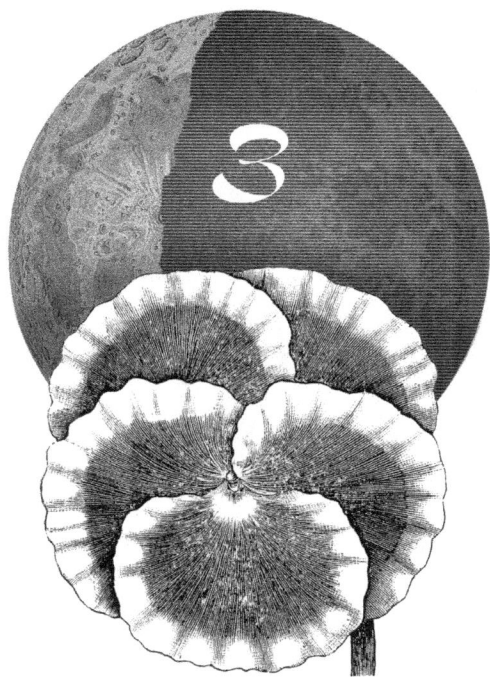

LATER POEMS

AFTERLIFE

When my soul has left this earth,
my happy bones laid to rest
among swaths of lily-of-the-valley—
a carnival of blooms—
I shall roam these very streets,
the grass of various retreats.
I've shed glycerin tears,
strewn countless sleeping pods of daisies
to awaken,
emerge the ghosts of me—
those I've known,
those I've yet to discover.

When being alive's akin to stasis,
a buzzing white noise
between birth and the ability to walk through walls,
I'll transcend this body and
revel in its luminescence,
like the gray glitter of rain
appears in a thicket of fog.
The perceptive among us
spy the inklings,
bubbles in our vision after staring at the sun,
shadows floating in my eye—
I have seen them always.

Perhaps you'll find me tending your garden,
gracing Florentine piazzas,
Scottish castles and English moors,
dining with Dorothy Parker,

Truman Capote, T.S. Eliot and Marianne Moore,
We'll debate the power of wit,
the gift of verse
and all the nonsense you do
when you've all the time in the world
to be the soul, person, or sentient being
you're truly meant to be:

A life without limits,
only in death.

WATCHING SCARY MOVIES

You make me want to spin the bottle
Mess around to Sonic Youth
You make me want to change the subject
Learn to speak in noise
You make me want to like November
Eat samosas late at night
You make me want to kiss the waitress
Take a bus to Alabama
Shake the city down for change
Chat with all the subway strangers
Do the things I never did
Stuff my face with purple play-dough
Wear your jacket in the lake
Finger-paint the master bedroom
Learn to be a kid

DEVIL BIRDS

we called them the Devil Birds.
their chatter like a chainsaw
trashing the stillness
of early-morning dark.
we called them the Devil Birds.
they were desperate for death—
a party, a weekend, a relationship,
a Tuesday night watching Scarface on loop.
all our pretend time
stashed in an eight-ball of coke,
fish-scale sold by Cleopatra.
she studied biology.
she made the best vegetarian burritos.
she hosted my 22nd birthday party.
she held my hand in public just because.

the Devil Birds begin their damage
at three or four in the morning—
at two o'clock in miserable March.
I think they were praying for spring,
maddening, undecipherable incantations
louder and louder they shouted!
even so we continued using—
talking, never listening,
telling, never sharing—
the usual things that cokeheads do.
at dawn I ran outside to swim in the gray,
a dense fog dragging its feet because it was a school day.
you grabbed your Polaroid,
snapped my photo:

my saucer eyes searching,
scattered, skittish.
there is loneliness,
profound, empty—
a deeper fear
scrawled across my face.

807

Blue is the evil eye,
the sacred,
the bereaved,
the hanged man with a noose necklace
pending a pine box.

Blue is the melody
thumping tracks thru America,
the creator,
the maker,
the god of all music.

Blue is Joni Mitchell's melancholy breath,
truest shade of darkness,
which is not black but inky blue,
slinking over hay bales,
the whispering corn
and that city highway
where the art of no feeling becomes habit.
In the end you're just as blue as those prison corpses
thrust in pine boxes.

Blue is the longest note I ever held.
You could cup it in your palm
and it'd blow you all away,
show you the shock,
the darkest side of the brain
awash in *Rhapsody in Blue*—
the Leonard Cohen hue.

Midnight is the color of fumbling souls,
ultramarine the Virgin's robes.

Blue is you and me,
the roiling surf,
background of storms and crackle lightning.
It is the sorrow of lost souls never meeting
and missing your lover.
Blue is the color of honesty
and for that, I am grateful.

SEARCHING

A relapse of the soul,
A rift, restart of the heart
From which we barter
For blessedness in wafers
And tendered time.

I search in rhymes
Of those who came before
Of Leonard, of Lou and Patti
And I'm told to pray, pray, pray
'cept I don't know what to say.
I only know the song of Bacchus's cup
And how to write petty letters
To those tentacle tethers
That pulls me to you.

If anything, I'm cruel in the day,
Sincere in the night
When there's little to light
To guide the ghosts
Hidden in the operating theatre
"Aetherized upon a table—"
Come Prufrock and prove me a humanity.

There are sins and there are struggles.
Am I to be Sisyphus?
Forever pushing boulders
Up hills in the road
Or Ophelia drowned from a broken branch?

The sinner is the saint,
The joker, the broker of a life unlived—
Everything I ain't
But could be in a cool blue pool of shade
Poured from some catwalk overhead.

I'll keep my knuckles white white rabbit white
And grind my salt to the earth
'Til the muddy reframe in my ears
Wreathes my crown with trampled daisies,

For I am young and I am old—
I'm colder still,
But I'll rest the night the best I can,
Let the ropy ink of blackness
Reap my dreams
And sow a future,
For I was destined for something, I'm sure

I was born a lioness of God—
Lear my cry,
Hear me roar—Count it—
1, 2, 3, 4...

JARDIN DES GENOUX (THE GARDEN OF KNEES)

Feed me your kneez
I am starved for them, pleaz!
Voracious, vicious
The sinew mew
Of muscle tied tendon—
A virtuous thing.

I'm a dark girl now,
I inhabit the xx,
Orchids—black and demolished
Brave in their nakedness
Spread on wood,
But ALL WRONG when cramped
In vase—trampled—
I'm in need of your kneez.

Blackish human flower blood
Fills finger paint pots,
Lipstick tubes
Stamps a gash
A cut of yellowed teeth.

I missed your birthday
It startled me—THE EAZ!
It's been a year of elbows,
Peachy down of inner thigh
But still, I need—
I drown in it,
I NEED THEM—
Baby, I'm in love wit dem kneez!

Will you feed them to me?
I may be a devil girl,
Yet still,
I aim to pleez.

*   *   *   *   *

Nourris-moi vos genoux

JUNKIE

Lou Reed's dead
And on I went,
Waiting
For
The
Man.

I'm all blown up
It isn't lovely
Needing a way
To touch base
With Slowed-Down
The slack-jawed liar,
Kicked down cracked
In the cripple cut
Of a convenient cosmetics mirror
Projecting...

Junk-Face,
Jailer of the soul,
Seeking body to inhabit,
Slouched on the bleached wood wall.

I stare them blotches
Blinking at me
Asking me to wait
At last run ragged,
Lunchtime in the Land of Hands Exchanging

I'm squinting
Stitching up this hand,
Arm, leg, foot, head, heart,
With threaded gut
Spun thin like string
It pulls me sick.
Sewn closed, I'm whole,
On loan for no one,
Waiting for none.
The horses, chained up.
Are braying at locked doors.

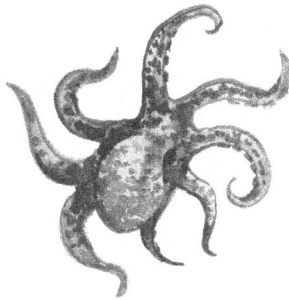

SYNTH

Electro-pop
The beats we covet now,
Amphetamines
In a time of nodding out
Like neon Pac Men under-fed,
They're studded with stick-on gems
Applied with speed
This visual appearance
Is ever-bending light—
Borrowed, careless, all remiss
I'm sharpening my knife.

At 23 we're cramming in
At 28 we're knocking out
I don't know anyone at all
Who isn't tugging at the plastic wrap.
The drugs we take
Make party all the time,
Long nails, bit tits,
A naked body fight,
But I'm attracted to the night,
All hail the Sister's greatest gift!
No dignity, a life that's stripped
A life along with every hit.

Stop testing me, I'm sick of it,
Stop testing me, you hear?
I'm sick of being someone's bitch,
This body here is mine to wreck.

I've got a ring where you can't see,
I'm married only straight to me.

I simply don't know how to write,
I don't know how to write at all!
Now slip that through the synthesizer,
A sound loop looping other loops,
The voice is mine, repeating noise
Withdrawn, diffuse, I'm keeping time.
The Experience of being Human,
Is neatly posed and packed away
All this time I've spent life screaming,
Increasingly unheard.

HOTEL CHELSEA

Is a big red brick
The Chelsea Hotel
Is how I know it now
Flush with phantom vapors
On 23rd Street
Between 7th and 8th
Where the living wandered out
And the dead still cling
Clink clink, clink to the rugged metal sinks.
I was moving to the city in 100 degrees

All I ever wanted was a room of my own
At the Hotel Chelsea
Where On the Road was born
Where Ginsburg tuned in, dropped out
Dee Dee and Sid sped up, smacked out
Patti, Robert, Jasper, Dylan
They paid the rent with gifted art

I tricked my way to room 100
The number hidden as another
To keep away all freaks like me
I lie in wait
The chance to take
A little bit of Sid for me.
I traced a finger tenderly
'Round Nancy's death-mask body leak
A brown and faded shadow stain
Where Sid sat silent
Rat-faced, sick
Perhaps he clutched the slickened blade
To mark a scar and make it stick

Floor one through twelve's a gallery
My hands, they hovered
I uncovered
Original Basquiats
Unique de Koonings
Now missing from the storied halls
Those shiftless aching orphan shells
Made it out now, after all

I felt it in those pulsing walls
The energy of artists seething
Work created and discarded
Like Andy's Viva leapt from the roof
Little canary flying
All dizzy in the chloroform breeze

Hotel Chelsea
The Chelsea Hotel
Collects the best
All thieves and con men
The tumult of creativity
And torture of addiction
Pain you keep stepping on
You politicians, policeman people
Rent-raisers, opportunity-takers
All artless destroyers of culture-makers
All I ever wanted was a room of my own
In the Hotel Chelsea
The Chelsea Hotel
Observe the ordinary
Absorb the extras
A carnival of souls
Now shuttered
A legendary love
Officially, eternally closed.

TO MY FATHER: THE GREATEST MAN IN THE WORLD

I cherish a snapshot of you and mom
bracing one another on an elephant's bedecked back,
India nipping at your heels,
unsteady in your footing, your fleeting smile
half worried, half excited.

Boy face grown older,
there is purity in the crinkles
napping on a blanket of soft skin.
Kind heart, kind hands
holding mine—
the smell of Ace Hardware on Sunday.
I hated that Pontiac.

Somehow we grew and still grow
Together,
sprung from adolescent quips,
now nurtured intellectual sparring—
always gentle, always wise.

Beyond the mold you built yourself,
mud, mortar, bricks—yourself,
lies a conductor of symphonies, sonatas
billowing in the wind on a summer's evening.
History buff learned, creative, sensitive,
You are lonely the way I am lonely—
a lovely stillness, the possibility we are misunderstood,
wink of a twinkled creasing eye.

Forever you will be tattooed on my chest,
collarbone, and yes it hurt,
meaning I, your Cherub,
appear in everything you are—
bones, skin, muscle, heart, brain—
Always near,
Always needing you,
Always her Daddy's girl.

CONCHAS CHINAS

Nothing's thicker than Darkness,
not even blood—animal or human.
Even though the Pacific is near
I see nothing hurtling through gentle waves
lapping, licking the tips of ancient rock people—
steadfast warriors claiming the sand.

Inky expanse of dripping dark,
watercolors married by a coffee stain,
in it I see loads of nothing
Made Animate—
Excitement and night spirits
fashioned like ghosts
poised beside like your naked face, mi amor.

This is Mexico singing
private prayers too privileged for light,
rearranging in shapes,
infinity pools, cabanas, the like.
Rosaries wound round wrists of old women,
off to chapel,
escaping the day's humorless clouds—
swaths of cotton spread like jam in blue
of daytime sky:
rainless, shadeless, shapeless—
no promise of Darkness and all its luxuries.

When night paints broad strokes,
stealing the sun,
townspeople grow dim,

faces indistinguishable from one another.
I draw stars with a Bic pen
exactly as I like them,
as frames—
the fringe of night
dotted with glowing orbs—
My design,
My delight.

FOR LORD BYRON, LOST AT SEA

In the sapphire waters of the Mediterranean,
I see the glint, a mop of curls,
a mess of shimmering brown.
Inchoate ideas flickering neurons in your brain.

Unabashed, you collect stories on shore
of catastrophe, the perils of romance,
charged as churning waves
yearning to tip your boat quivering,
hostile and lovely before a lightning storm.

How I wish I knew thee,
Boy of the Night and its pleasures.
I forever search in artists,
musicians and the like,
seeking for you in your poems
fraught with the pain of youth plundered.

Laudanum pupils, an opiate glow—
The elegance of youth transformed.
"And thou are dead, as young and fair,"
And thou art dead, Lord Byron,
yet alive in the confines of my dreams
wrapped as gift.
Torn apart by hungry fingers—
the surprise of your parcel
different each time.
Your tragic beauty informs me,
consumes me,

instructs me to write,
though my musings hardly do you justice.
Sometimes I wonder—
your spirit sails the sea,
Never to be found.
Lost to me.

ADDICTION/RECOVERY

Ripples curling, tumbling—
lacy seaweed crashing,
gossamer-like,
on silver moon sand.

My body floats in night water
beyond the struggle to shore.

Marina animal-filled ears
like a liquid cotton,
Narcotic in Persistence,
Opiate in Stillness,
letting the Atlantic bathe,
soothe my milk body.
My coated honey eyes are drifting rafts.
Awake/Asleep/Neither.
Perfection is in the lack.

If just for a moment,
I am embalmed.
The horror and euphoria of chasing
Ephemera—bridge of gauze
veiling a porcelain face.
Bloodless, blood let to drip,
to saunter slowly
until it meets a cut as real—
it enters, inhabits.

When I wake,
crushed roses

smatter chalk cheeks.
There is no bliss,
save for in sleep,
I am alive.
I am alive!
And so,
I am allowed to dream,
to tussle with bliss,
awake, and be.
Me.

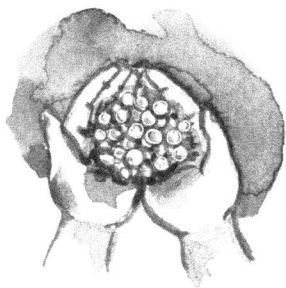

SELF-TITLED POEM #3

Champagne curls trapped in a brush
sink-side, glittered gold reflected—
The mirror: Curls on forehead,
skimming shoulders round and proud.
Large arms.

Porcelain skin scattered—
freckles here,
freckles there,
disappearing,
reappearing,
Here, not There.

My eyes are colors peeled like onions:
Pupils black, gold circle,
gilt green watercolor wash,
ring of blue or grey,
day to day.

Blip of a nose,
Grandma's cherub lips like wings,
breasts well formed,
two pale peaks,
held high and shapely,
pink pert nipples.
These, my tits, the color of me.

Sloping belly on the shrink,
large legs, marble-carved and

long, long toes,
nails dripped in chocolate red.

Large span of piano hands
mixing makeup,
marking my face,
My Clan, kohl eyes
rimmed and greener today.

The memory of finger painting,
Mommy's Estée Lauder and Chanel
not lost, genetics too—
Those I carry, Those I don't.

This soft span of skin, a deviant.
Breasts too large, too light,
anomaly of curls.
Italian appetite, Irish looks, German build,
Eastern European, half my heritage.
Unique oddness of mood, afflictions—
Me, the image projected,
Mimicking slump of left hip.

"Rubenesque" with an elfin face,
mismatched body,
muddled identity to correct,
repair,
make proportioned,
refine.
I have been confined.
Nine men stole it, broke it,
hung it in the hall,
My skin, the wall.

For the first time,
I'll take this body:
all its limits,
possibilities,
fates,
facts,
hate it,
love it,
some beast in-between—
I'll take This Body
and make it Mine.

LION-HEART

It's a kind of human condition
when we seek the Lotus-Eaters.
We meet them at the blunt end of earth
or mid sea among the white-tipped sharks
smacking lips for a drowning man.

You will not sink,
not an inch or three.
Head full of do-ins and concepts:
Rationality. Logic. "Safety."
Socially acceptable, Perfect-even Posh.

This thing we call coal—
diamonds,
miles and miles of diamonds
burrowed in a hole.
the soil-filled soul.

Whatever bones you bury,
I'll dig up.
Though you're a man of many ruses,
I'm a woman with excuses
and I've made them all.

So I will find your heart
as it's soldered to mine.
I am reminded that
"there but for the grace of God go I."

A JOB TO DO

February in Manhattan is grim—
it has been since the recession.
Once again I am "jobless,"
without "Job,"
without Paycheck,
precious paper dolls they are.

Mediums rotate with winter shadows.
That nice lady on TV,
perfect bob, capped teeth, twitchy smile:
Snow Snow Snow!
Collective sigh of despair.
But I work.

I work early mornings,
cold nights snow-scattered.
The simple act of pen to page,
cutting and pasting,
arranging, glittering or framing,
YES, I am busy this February
taking the world
underground-up.

I am a poet.
I write images from a rotating gallery,
Projections—mind to paper—
tickled with every color glitter and texture
in Martha Stewart's ultimate glitter collection
that I bought on the Home Shopping Network.
You'll find my paillettes

sparkling in sewer drains,
so as not to sully carpets and couches
with gleaming detritus when I visit.
My name, etched in Sharpie
on a naked wall yearning to be touched
by Permanence.
Signatures, riddles, rhymes—
all Valentines—
From me to New York City,
or to you, just you.
These small-scale wonders
I have made, really,
belong just to you.

FOR SIDNEY VICIOUS

Wisp of tail keeping balance,
You topple candles, odds, ends,
glasses in which we share our seltzer
become broken shards scattered—
Your glass menagerie—
and so we use plastic cups.

Your paws bat around bits of string
when not warming my palms,
kitten hands slipped into mine.
White noise of television fizzles.
You stretch your little body over mine,
tiny heart beating two for my every one.

We know us,
practice reading feelings,
cartography—mapping emotions.
Your fuzzy head rests
television-towards,
but we see only one another,
sharing, educating.

Your curling, limber body
blankets my sorrows.
My tears, beads of dew marring your fur
like when you splash around,
enjoying the remnants of my recent shower.
Dancing bravely, leaping surface to surface,
You, my prince, are a picture of true love.

NEW ORDER

Octopus overcomes New York City
skimming an obsidian sea—
street signs mired in liquid onyx—
we're blind.
I, in a boat of frozen winter trash
flick chrysoberyl eyes,
gold-green, cat-like eyes
glinting, shiny as marbles.

These sidewalks are smashed gilt
crushed and ravaged by wayward tentacles.
The media, in desperation, worries.
"This Octopus may be a Squid,"
Media angles are sickly sharp,
jagged Lego pieces
split under the foot of an infant culture
to which I belong.

We, these newborn,
slink and slug pen ink,
fluid as the cephalopod's moody spillage
marking streets, now canals,
where I and my contemporaries
lift litter fished from sewers,
drainpipes,
corner puddles that never seem to dry,
to build an edifice to Those That Came Before,
nurtured this Art in swaddling clothes.
The city drowns in Octo-Squid
sucking us up—

(though it's been happening for years)
to swat us into the East River,
where neither Brooklyn nor Queens can save us.
Welcome to the First World gone Third.

Can't afford paper?
I have skin.
Join my boat and I'll gladly share.
Vive la revolution,
let the words flow,
thwart these New New York tentacles—
it's time we run the fucking show.

SEPIA

The curious tone of a torn photograph.
An Italian wedding, circa 1893,
where the happiest day isn't gray
and tastes like a hand-rolled
Sicilian cigar. Synesthesia—

hard to record yet hard to forget.
Sepia boy running his tongue,
dew lips that kiss his pillow—
we thought them stories,
not prayers,
to keep your soul asleep—
you body, too.

For soon it'll be you,
a jagged ripple of photo paper
perforated,
your wedding, your seed,
to sow and sweep with speed.

FIRST BLUSH

It's faux spring in February.
Little birds, chirping and confused,
flit from naked bony finger of branch
to chalk-white window sills
slathered with spent meals of pigeons
made an ashy shadow by the season's
Abundant Snow.

I've shed my cashmere for a summer dress
set with black lace binding the bust—
color of eggshells stepped-on,
mashed to a cotton paste reformed—
This dress poking through

smells like vetiver,
patchouli, tuberose and black plum,
the skin of which ripples at the slightest touch.
Small krill flip themselves,
disguised as small stones, to mark the pool
swirling at the bottom of a whispering creek—
its secrets leached like minerals

spelled on base boards bearing
"POST NO BILLS,"
where a deli on 14th and Avenue A
stood before the fire.
Now bits of wooden ash fly at my eyes.
In this imitation spring breeze
I swear I can see budding leaves
slowly reaching for fabricated air.

I wish so painfully,
feel so deeply, that I should
Bloom and drink the sun too,
to be happy, to be Spring,
to be naked and real like Whitman—
the nature of the city,
the nurture of the shore—
and what it's like to hold the Two
like my kitten's paw, sharp and soft.

Pigeons preen their feathers
for a spring that's not to come
'til winter's loosened grip prods me,
pries me open,
awake and receptive,
as any ordinary bulb, leaf,
flower, tree,
and I can ride my boat to Whitman
where he will gather me.

A TWITTER POEM #1: SUMMER, 5 YEARS OLD

Cicadas sticky in summer sap
Stuck to the driveway, wings amuck,
I said the Sh'ma, crawled into bed.

LAVENDER

is the most beautiful hue
buried in the color spectrum.
Warms like a blanket,
tastes as it looks—
I could stare at it for hours
and never grow bored,
like when I'm with you.

We press our hearts together
to transfer the data of feeling,
sharing everything,
saying nothing—
lost in the subtle color of a kiss.

A MEMORY REPEATING

I'm missing pieces of you today,
even though you are only pieces.
Whitish, soft sand dunes
sifted through mucosal
membranes, eyeball, lung, throat.
Acid acts make right the process
to process the chemical properties—
this alchemy, an oncology of the soul.
The mix is brackish,
fully ratcheted and scaly-backed,
clicked up like an Epi Pen:
Enter the Fix. These tricks,
neither happy nor unhappy,
Just sad, the gladdest kind of sad there is.
These thoughts are curious,
coming and going.
Though I am well,
they'll shriek from time to time,
buckle my knees
and send me on my way.

THIS IS A SOUL SONG

I was born with a broken heart,
two moons stitched in its place.
The synthetic childhood
of a syrup-spun fantasy—
I built a barricade of marbles
rolling hard and deep to keep me
safe.

Doctor, wake me when you're done.
Do I have a heart to speak?
Am I free of these demons
that pray at the bottom of my shoes
in the dim light of a child's bedroom?
I've seen them watching me
since I was only eight.

This anesthesia
feeding on the wires of my brain
doesn't feel like much,
but it's good, fuzzed-out,
says I can do it alone,
this fallen fool—
though all of us,
even you,
are junkies and tools.

My life is bittersweet,
I won't forget this pain
but I'll share it with you:
trace these scars to see

the stars scattered
like spent embers smoldering,
searing the flesh.

Forgive me both father and mother
for I have sinned,
but so have they, and in a darker way.
At least I can say I've learned my name,
and No One,
not even them,
can take that away.

BALENCIAGA PARIS

Moss, Violet, Sandalwood—
all notes in my favorite perfume—
tastes like emboldened bark,
a primeval tree thrust like a knife
aglitter, filtering shades of sun in shadows
to blanket and thicken the forest floor.

The subway jangles.
There's a new Cars song
detailed in my Rolling Stone,
pages my fingers flip,
every flick slinging the scent—
Moss, Violet, Sandalwood—
singing through the tinny train:
an ancient Bavarian wood
shot through this paper city
of paper people. Paper hearts
record the scrawlings of a wild beat.

I recall a History Channel special
where nature devours deserted cities
vine by vine, spiders, mice.
Bridges built by clever men
crumble and fall,
become lush and green.
And we'll be clean cultivating souls,
letting them breathe—
Moss, Violet, Sandalwood—
the essence of Me bound in the trees,
rustling along from leaf to leaf.

TO MY PUSSYCAT

I am blessed to know
the gem that is your spirit,
the cat-scratch of your voice
asking me to fix you an amaretto, when I was only 12.

Each stitch of your laughter,
a pearl of a story.
Your famous troublemaking kindness,
the makeup and Uncle Ace's face.

No matter the celebration:
birthdays, Christmas, or just because,
I can remember your stately bosoms and big heart
festooned with ribbons and bows (no one dared throw theirs away).

Your brightness, a star I see
even in a Manhattan night,
New York remembers you forever, Aunt Claudia,
and so do all of us in this room.

Though we have to give you up
to that great bar in the sky,
you're in great company, my rose.
and, if you save me a rye Manhattan,
someday, I'll see you there too.

I love you forever and ever, Aunt Claudia.

Love,
Ariel

26 AND NOT DYING

It's clear I'm not like everybody else when my roommate scuffles across the floor refusing her cane, when I can walk freely without hunching over, without bearing my ribs like bars on a cage—the cage we're in reflected on a chest that bears over seventy years of pure neuroses, naked and screaming as the child I appear to be.

You can't see my ribs because I'm fleshy like a woman and she's a skeleton and stinks like death. You can see my tattoo, an imprint of a cherub surrounded by stars floating, beautiful and marring my flesh, a symbol of my father's love, the desire to hurt and the will to die at any moment before I discovered recovery and it's many crevices creeping.

My first two roommates died on me, both on day one. Welcome to the Geriatric Ward, said a young woman that looked like Dallas and smelled stale as all the dead gardens in the world—a potpourri to mask the ever present scent of decay and old women shitting in their diapers or in their beds, demented men, painting the walls with urine.

Chronic Pain Disorder Unspecified, Severe Fibromyalgia, Myofascial Pain Syndrome—all of these and I need my Dilaudid every three hours and I scream a holy scream but the nurses are deaf to me. I can't open my hands and so I cry. I can't write because my hands are cramped up, my soul pouring out in the salt licks stemming from my eyes.

They are grotesque in a position only released by injections and medication. Medication that will have to wait until Mrs. Rodriguez gets her shit cleaned up. Medication that will have to wait until Mr. Holt gets a new glass of water. Medication that will have to wait until I grow old and find death peeking over my shoulder as I comb white strands of hair in the mirror, if I bother to comb it at all.

I'm the only one who showers, though the water's cold and feels like paintball pellets and so nobody notices me when I walk by as I am marked by no stench. I'm the pain in the ass who asks for nothing save for my pain injections every three hours while the rest of the ward howls every minute, every hour, every day for more water, new diapers, new family, more friends, new doctors, new, new, new. I just want the old me back. Do I have to shit myself to get it?

THIRTEEN WAYS OF LOOKING AT GLITTER

I
Mirrors reflecting nothing
but one another
I was lost in the glitter

II
What I thought was glitter
seemed rays of morning light
before I reached down to touch sun-stricken snow

III
The glitter in these Caribbean waters
of gentle cerulean blue
from so far away as our hotel room
was merely sand suspended in waves

IV
I smashed a beer bottle to pieces
to hear its sound reverberate
to make the room shake
and all I could find
was glitter instead of dust

V
A child's unfinished art project
hangs askew on a single father's fridge
dripping ill-applied glitter
into the dog bowl
where Watson will lap up the plastic beauties
and catch them in his whiskers
where he'll don them like earrings

VI

A sniff of smack
a hit of crack
she's making up her face
and all she can think about
is how much glitter a girl can wear
without looking like she's on drugs

VII

What is it about a drag queen's dress
that catches the corner of an eyelash
just a flash
as she belts a Judy Garland classic
It's glitter
and not just the craft kind
but the kind that comes from
a decorated soul

VIII

I painted my nipples pearly pink
brushed with layered glitter
I meant to turn you on
to make your day
after the stock markets closed
and you staggered home way past ten

IX

A child of five pointed skyward to the stars
and just knew that's where glitter lived

X

The Neue Galerie is one of my favorite places to be
I love the harsh lines, exaggerated emotions
of an Egon Schiele

but most of all, the glitter
of a golden Klimt
makes me hungry for goulash
they serve
in the café downstairs
only when it rains

XI
I feel love in cheap, plastic glitter
though I know love isn't cheap at all

XII
Heaven and hell may not exist
but glitter does

XIII
Not everything illuminated by glitter is lovely
and so we see things we don't want to see
but there is truth in it
that scintillates
and we are drawn to it
like a mirror fractured
broken, yes
but free

WHY CHILDREN SHOULD READ

I have always felt taken by a book—
the smell—flipping pages under my nose
to make alive a scent particular to
an author,
a story
a scene
a poem.

I read before I walked,
or maybe after,
but certainly before
I learned to operate the television,
before which I set the turntable
to Tchaikovsky
and danced,
my tutu
a flower,
a powder puff,
a marshmallow.

To read as a child
is to map your future.
You may be a poor drug-addict
starving, turning tricks,
but you'll be richer in mind
and able to jot your sorrows,
haphazardly cobbling works of art.

To not read, you avoid.
You watch and consume,

waste and assume the world
with hands that haven't imagination.
A big house and fancy cars means little
to a man who can't appreciate
the jokes his Yale interns
will tell at his expense
within earshot.

A child that reads
is a child tabula rasa
with the capability
to take her neatly laid palette
and perfect teardrop spread of paints,
to ditch the brush and say
Fuck it! And smear the whole mess
all over her face.

Art lives in books
and people too.
Without people,
there is no art.
Without art,
there is no culture.
Without culture,
there isn't jack shit.

And that's why children
should read books.

SELF-TITLED POEM #4

My childhood rooms smells
of old woman's lace-work cheek—
Grandma's White Linen worn heavy,
rich like speckled fat in the imported mortadella
we used to share
before Pain became my body,
which then became a vegetable garden,
lush with heirloom tomatoes odd in shape and color,
bursting bell peppers and Italian kale,
because I find it less offensive.

These black and brackish waters
run deep and still as cut glass
where once they tumbled, troubled,
now the sparkle of little star bodies
stretch their legs—spider webs on the surface.

Leaning into authenticity
is a privilege earned:
Collected through the old leather stink of books,
of floral silks and motorcycle boots
an undying appreciation of early punk rock,
The Organic Grill's eggless egg-salad club sandwich
and the courage to say goodbye to a lover
who doesn't agree.

FAIRYTALE

The hideous gnash of metal on metal
and I'm bludgeoning my own bruised skin,
when it's your sword cutting deep against my cheek;
its rusty blade's lip sips thimbles of burgundy blood
trickling in easy streams slithering from my neck.

I wear my chain mail like silk chiffon—
naked tracelings of latticework webs
that tumble, whispers, down warrior legs.
And the sisterly snakes of blood you drew,
I've made me a crown,
matting gilt blond tresses spectacularly red.

I won't be put underground in dead earth
like some iron casket nesting doll treasure
to be dug up by schoolboy pirates
or curious dogs.

I won't let me murder me
or you bury this:
It's a new kind of war, baby,
with all the same risks.

MONSTERS

These creatures make imprints in the dark.
Our memories captured
in pictures
are snapped by
swashbucklers

searching for monsters
and mists

in the cruel stillborn
early morning hours.

I'm sensitive to their
shadows as my own.

The inkblot beings
creeping closely

are blind and tend to
tangle with the rafters,

to end as paper
streamers dangling

like felons from the
gallows of a public
hanging.

My eyes are orbs
strangled in their
sockets
but the searing chafe
around my neck's a
ribbon.

Braided strands of
carnelian and cinnabar

mimic the sanguine
horror of what could
have been

had I not seen my
breath swirling high-
art patterns
in the cooling air
pooled by nighttime
curiosities.

They say everyone's
hiding from a monster,

or fighting to slay some
immortal beast.

But when you're tucked
into a lifetime as I am,
with a revolving
gallery of ghouls,

I'm never far from the
terror

that keeps me alive and
near to myself.

(And though life is
more complicated in the dark)

I am whole, complex, complete.

TATTOO

The raven's onyx feather drips
viscous drops connecting
meniscus to meniscus in an arc
under the safety of jutted rock collarbone—
a refuge in the constant dulling downpour
of murky late-summer sky.

The arcs become a system of crescents,
moon-like in their phasing,
from a bitten silver waxing full.
They are raised in scar like Braille,
over which my fingers fumble,
reading a Cherub with a wand of stars
magnetically charged in a thunderous storm.

This body of mine is magic
It scintillates in glints of pin-prick blood and heals
as the needle cobbles in and out,
spinning ink and the map of my spirit.
The mystical cartographer sketches
in an alabaster plot of skin
near that vital organ that beats and beats—
some call it a heart,
I call it my book—
it's where my story is.

SNOWBIRD

sings, sifting snow
shaken from a stately
Evergreen collapsing,
mutable shapes making
water weight-flakes,
paper doll cutout cousins
cloth clusters and tinsel things—

This Being—

a dove in opera gloves,
masquerades as if on stage,
illegally awake.

Swan dive,
crown-to-thighs,
the buoyancy of cotton sky
soothes her sulphur songs long sung,
those elegies in minor keys,
buried in her feathered chest—
all kindling for the snowbird's nest.

ORIGIN OF A SPECIES 10.31.11

The Electric Woman wears
wallpaper prints—

Darwin's Galápagos sketched on
silk

half-remembered
like Tennyson's Lotos-Eaters
in a laundanum laze.

She grieves Victoriana
where dust motes collect Fabergé eggs,
takes day-glo pills and fizzy tonics,
trails rainbow footprints in rivers when she goes.

Her skeleton is a system of channels
inlaid with chrysoberyls and alchemical magic:
An Impressionable Expressionist Smudge of the Contemporary
    Feminine:
The Electric Woman *en forme*
writes poems,
spins letters to God in imagist depictions.

Her words are lawless gardens of decapitated dandelions,
verse scrawled and loosely writ
with the blood of a thousand celery sticks
on abandoned stretches of meat market walls
where even the butchers won't butch after dark.

In an era of newly impossible days,
the poet *must* effloresce,
fickle in her particular way.

HOVER

Strange inhabitants
these music-makers of the mind find
when curtains playing woodland patterns
on a window lounge apart
to greet another early darkness:

The hush of winter hidden in the pines.

A SHITTY POEM FOR ADAM

Many nights
you climbed in a furrow
deep in rib—
the rib of Eve.
Cuz I'm the one
who made you Adam,
took you in,
your shiny eyes
filled with kindness—
a terrific blindness
rare these days.

You loved my thighs
in a pinup pose,
a snapshot of the Bahamas
with watered down rum.
Yet you put me down
knocked me 'round
when I needed you.
I think you needed me too.

We imagined a house in the Valley,
our kids, some cats,
your German Shepherd,
sipping Manhattans
till the sun took cover
deep beneath summer clouds.
It was a lonely lead-glass dream
so it seems, as I was the only one dreaming.

Where's your soul been hiding?
Where's that spine?
Lifted out the back like a big red lobster
ready for a bath of butter?
When you shacked up with a lucky Kentucky
you forgot how to be a friend,
forgot how to take a stand.
It's a two-way traffic lane my baby
and I'm sick of all the pain,
sick of stumblin on yellow tape.

When you chose to let me leave
New York without a word,
you left our friendship,
forgot my birthday,
our time together,
our seven-year ride.
You owe me your voice on the line.

But you're nothing but a big old coward
standing in that great girl's shadow
who called me toxic, a junkie a loser—
where for fuck's sake were you?
You've finally done me,
you done it, you won,
cash in your tokens
for a lifetime of fun
as you cheat, lie and fake your way—
the way you know best since the day you arrived.

I loved you twice, as a lover then a friend
But it's the latter that stings the most.
You've let me down
below the ground,

too many times for far too long.
Someday you'll be
trapped in a dead-end marriage
while I write my way to fame.
This poem may be shitty
But it's all for you my baby—
Tell me:
Why you gotta be so mean?

ESCAPE PLAN

Hieronymus
Bosch is here for
tea,

His sinners 'n
creatures

All stuck in my
teeth.

We debate the
taste of sulfur,

Of Seurat and
storytelling,

The
chromosomal
makeup of
orchids

And love in a
world of chains.

This new brand
of hell

Swells—
unexceptional.

The drone of the dead
Passes for prayers
In the tabernacle of life,
Of light and reprieve.

Your lover's a killer,
Your assassin—your saint
The structure of badness—
Perdition dispersed.

Who make it now break it,
This slip of a soul,
Now holds tight.
I won't take it,
Won't fake it,
But I'll make it baby,
I will.

MANIFESTA 2

i wear the boots of the suffering.
to suffer is to traverse
the human condition,
to descend the spine's ladder
punched fulla holes
where memory threads
swing like holiday ornaments.
the barest tree
in the big, bad forest
has bulbs that blink 'n blind
'n blue, red, white out/the right out.
under a moon's candle gaze
i'm a beast in the dark.
wanna make it better?
make it in leather,
i'll don that skin
and break it in.
here's to the anti-maiden
drunk on mirth!
from that mineral earth
where diamonds slumber
far below.

IT'S CHRISTMAS IN LONDON

Fingers of dead oak
massage midnight psalms and prayers,
wind-whipped in a smudge of sky.

It's Christmas Eve.
Religious tourists clamor:
the stained glass candle-lit doors of the devout.
And I, just passing by,
crackle pockmarked snow icily under foot.

Flakes fall in moody drifts.
A sleepy littering of celestial glitter dwindles.
The frenzy of stars scatter and stick,
dimming in late-night slate.

Draped in melancholy,
a dove-grey dawn tempers the shimmering nightscape.
A fractal memory is captured—
static as a photograph.

AFTER THE RECESSION

There is a peculiar loveliness
in decapitated orchids,
their stamens stuck out,
inky tentacles seize flower heads.
THE KRAKEN
devouring the ship!
I collect wrecks in a fish tank.

There is glory in decay—a beauty—
when decay is decorum,
institution,
the fundamentals—
great leaps never landed.
Everyone wears knee supports from Walgreens,
takes Bayer for no heart attacks,
takes prayer for no Hell.

Each day is new language,
new legend of signs & systems.
The stethoscopes dripping from our necks
are no longer useful,
no longer hear sound
of one heart humming to another.

When life breaks down,
rusts, grows musty,
why do we turn the same keys?
Type the same codes?
VIRUS HAS BEEN DETECTED—
ACCESS DENIED.

A MEDITATION

GRIEF is an electronic loop
throws you back like a sucker-punch
raw, warm,
right in the ribs
where breath becomes blood
& blood is reel-time
tek-ni-kolor
a Hershey's/food-dye drip
corn syrup
in tex-chure it drags
zig-zags littered tears
line...blip...blip line blip...
a heart monitor
flatlines

I meditate in Ray Bans
those Risky Business Wayfarers
in which I manage
business that is risky
because I see everything
abject: apart from, outside of
a placenta separating
& unattached
I EAT IT LIKE JELLO
one, two three...

come hear my dead girls
come little darlings
let me wade in your wide river
you drowned women bobbing
all mistresses

mismanaged & discarded
clutching bloody valentines
furtively in hand

in your names
I tack prayer flags
little ladders that scale
the Buddhist monastery
carved in Huangshan's neck
they are wiry ivy
climbing skyward to Nirvana
& other places
absent from maps
in Absentia
you are fully present
& I see you
lugging carpetbags to heaven
you bear the weight of our guilt

in GRIEF
we keep stones in our shoes
because
we remember
& because
we cannot forget

A DECLARATION OF EXISTENCE

Oh Mama, Dear Daddy,
Your little girl's a sinner.
I count my sins,
Those matchstick men
Affixed to the wall
Above my bed
Lined neat, toy soldiers
Always overhead.

Though I haven't slept
In quite some time:
I am clear,
This is an age of artlessness,
Producer here is God,
The artist, a beggar counting change,
Somehow
We got terribly turned around.

This whisper smoke
Of cigarettes
Nicked from the corner store,
Curls, serpent-like
From kitten lips
Unfurling little prayers.

Cajoling my cat's tawny fur
Through a snip of finger tips,
I'm reminded of that schoolyard bit:
"Here is the church, here is the steeple,
Open the doors"
I'm a fox among people.

I experiment with states of consciousness
While courting conscientiousness
From civil sergeants
Serving lives I'll never have,
Will never see the inside of
Will never really want.

I beat the drum of Baudelaire,
Turgenev, Tolstoy,
The New York Few,
Rachmaninoff slings moody notes against the wall
Slapped like paper cut-outs
Feeling one another out
Under the guise of dark.

The life I've chosen comes up lonely
But I've got friends along my path,
Musicians making secret records,
Writers slumped against the wall,
Painters bruising measure strokes
In the United States of Digitalia.

I'm a poet
Cuz I say so.
It's an age where words are truth.
When I die I'll be a vesper
Tumbling through the ether,
But I'll always be remembered
Cuz of all I've writ.

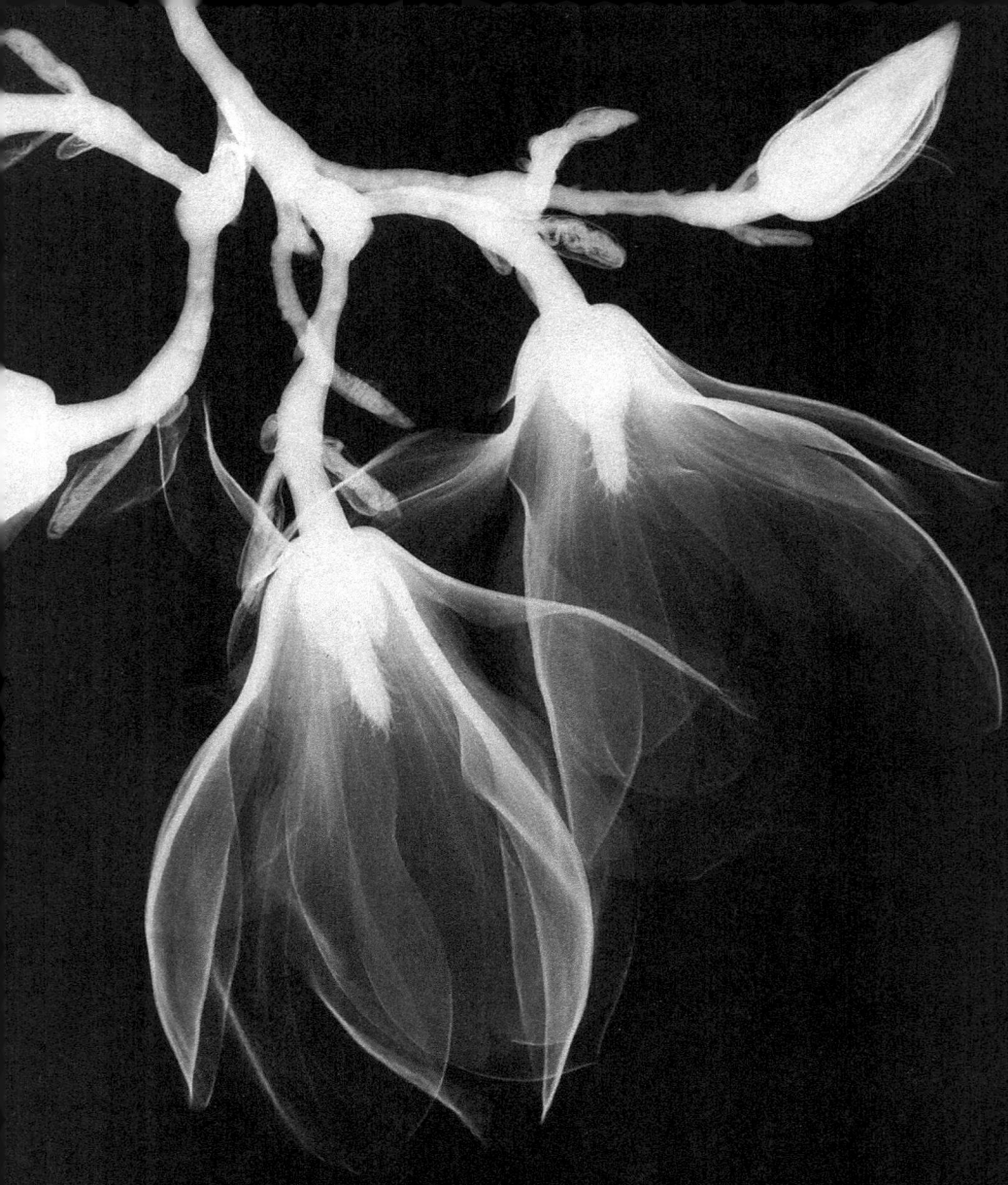

ARIEL JASTROMB   COLLECTED POEMS

LIGHTING UP THE SEE

VOLUME II

BLACKBIRD
ARTS PRESS

TABLE OF CONTENTS

INTRODUCTION

WHILE ARIEL'S MEDIUM was the written word, she derived inspiration from all her senses and multiple artistic channels. She drew from life's experiences—the beauty, tragedy and emotional power of the world around her. Her essence as an artist was her unwavering devotion to her craft, her acute empathy towards others and her desire to embrace the unknown while fueling her curiosity.

Her gifts are evident in her poetry. Her passion, warmth, wisdom and deep-rooted sensitivity are captured by her reflections and themes.

I had a firsthand glimpse into this precocious artist during her formative years and as she matured into a young woman. Ariel had her demons that manifested themselves from time to time, adding dimension to her work.

Ariel and I connected through her curiosity of music and art. She had an openness and thirst to know more than just the dilettante observer. Her tastes went beyond the bands of her generation, like the Cure, Clash and others. Her interest was more than the flavor of the day. She reveled in absorbing music as a social and cultural phenomenon; how this sonic poetry moved generations from the time the first notes were played and the first captivating words were uttered. Ariel would have relished being a part of music scenes she was excluded from by chronology.

Our vibrant and extensive conversations touched on jazz, pop, gospel and soul; nothing escaped her musical horizons. Some of our most animated conversations revolved around the influence of rap, blues and rock on punk, her beloved style. For Ariel, punk captured the spirit and rage of her generation. It was a musical style one would not think appeals to a hyper-sensitive poet, but Patti Smith was her touchstone. This eclectic and far reaching musical and artistic palette was what made this free-thinking, impassioned artist who she was.

I miss our discussions. Ariel's warm heart, sarcastic sense of humor, individual fashion sensibility (a whole other topic) and intelligence will be her legacy.

These pages provide a glimpse into this complex artist. Of course, not the entire story, but the one that remains to savor and enjoy.

—PHILIP REALMUTO

CINDY SHERMAN SERIES

These poems are inspired by a particular period of Cindy Sherman's work. They do not, in any way, reflect the artist's intention. They are purely inspiring for me. The practice of writing based on a picture or work of art is called ekphrasis. *I write what the women portrayed in her photographs may be thinking or living. The poems are written from my experience viewing Sherman's art.* —A. J.

OPHELIA REALIZED

"Envole-toi bien lion de ces miasmes morbides;
Va te purifier dans l'aire superior."—Baudelaire

Far from the country stream—
asphalt seemed a blank canvas.
You jumped from a rickety balcony,
painted with black orchids you birthed.
They were your children blooming.

A thrilling drop, desperate dark swan,
makes Art on Avenue B.
Fresh concrete, sticky,
Bubbling in the heat—
Your silhouette splashes the street
spilt blood trailing your halo.

Your diamonds for eyes—
they turned to dust when you fell.
Now a shimmering blanket sweeping,
Protecting you,
Protecting your madness.

The dress you wore,
A Victorian royal blue,
lounges in my closet
for your daughter, who weeps black tears,
just as yours.
You'll never meet.

Yet the fearless child breathes real air,
Wrest from your own womb.
She will never know your radiance,
Gratitude, gentle love, fragility.

Your *Times* obituary,
remains taped to your daughter's wall.
Porcelain face, sharp tongue—
Magnificent portrait glittering,
now worn, her hands studying repeatedly
the contours of your smile

Dark Ophelia, do you hear her prayers?

GLORIA

Child of the Night
matches light
moths dueling for flame
The tender age of seventeen.

Glowing crimson cigarette—
beacon in the dark—
crawls through sultry summer
unfurling coils of smoky plumage,
thrust among bezel-set stars
Winking.

You shot him in the chest,
bedroom littered with shells,
lashes catching fine tears.
No more rag doll, No more punching bag
Nowhere to go.

The flick of your cigarette,
now here, now there,
now pure Relief?
Key carrier, your brain scribbles,
resembling an Escher print,
with continual stairs to climb.
One foot and then the other
to catch that train called Freedom.

Pacing a silent run, stumbling along the way,
You leave a half-life for one full of journeys,

anywhere else but here.
Back turned, shoes clicking down the road,
I see the red tip of your cigarette disappear,
consumed by the cloying sickness of fog.

A PARK AVENUE CONFESSION

Forgive me father for I have sinned,
I loathe the man who married me.
Ivory silk dress, hand-stitched pearls
ripped from my dress,
a futile gesture,
expression of pain and lack of hope.
Stained with chlorine tears,
defiled, I've punished it to the linen closet
amongst rags and soiled tea towels.
Come nightfall, I dream of crimson
roses smashed upon your white, white walls—
blood spattered like torn petals.
Cleaning, cooking,
forgettable, regrettable sex
saved for the tart who wears my mink.
Spilt dirty martinis, Seconals numbing,
fearful of the rising sun.
Tender sleep, my only joy.
He snores, grunts boar-like,
pokes at me—
curled fetus at the end of the bed.
I pretend to sleep.
Do you hear my prayers?
Are they tempered by thick moulded walls?
He drinks, wets the bed,
pissing himself
Pissing On Me.
Fooled me, fooled the priest,

day comes—a violent storm
I make his tea,
biding time,
wasting mine.

POUGHKEEPSIE PIN-UP

Waxen leaves cleave, primordial trees
under marshmallow clouds you cycled,
bare feet, scraped knees—
suburban calloused balls of feet and heels—
peddling everywhere fast.

Flaxen hair flying face-ward in the wind,
the glitter of New York and all it means,
just a train away!
Poughkeepsie's for small time suckers,
chomping on a lollipop,
Someday they'll see.

Even in a crumbling Hell's Kitchen apartment,
roaches scattering through the night,
You water peonies, begonias and lilies with affection.
The precious blooms burst, competing for light,
lined as tin soldiers saluting the windowsill.

The Excitement, burning desire to be Loved,
Noticed, emerald dust flitting in your eyes.
From girl to woman, captured
carefully by a camera's lens,
the man behind rummaging in his trousers—
So nubile, so fresh!

Your flesh a canvas on which to spin stories,
little dolls with budding breasts.

First satiny shot and youth exposed—
Remember schoolboys lifting
40 oz. malt liquor from the gas station,
grass-stained shoes?

Your body floats,
belonging, if for just a moment, to Him,
His lens lounging,
tracing the map of your figure on crinkled sheets.

Several snaps all in a row,
flashes like lightning bugs from the family garden,
cradled in glass jars, straining to breathe,
striving to escape the monotony of struggling.

Welcome to New York, Kiddo.
It's all upwards from here.

BODY SNATCHER

I've never done this before.
Chugging train from
somewhere

Delaware deposited,

a fun house of mirrors

stretched out and then squat
at times.

He said he'd make me a man.

I flatten this sliver of figure,

make sweepable under plush
carpets

burying toes with fuzz,

Sneaking from one edge to

another Completely.

Is this how boys dress?
Or am I a man?
Can you help me be
what the Delaware sea told
me?

Sand dollars shackled in tin
red bucket prison,
plunked one after the other.

I, child of a forgotten coast,
missed the boat
floating summer ringlets,
two-piece tops ruffling—
little girls. I need no top.

I am king of all wild things!
Dronning drugs at the disco.
You gathered me up—
great big sails for arms.
You said you'd make me a man
only if I knew what it meant,
that dressing boy-like wasn't enough—
I had to make room for you.

Your indelible print.
I feel it always now,
even when you're far-flung,
drunk on daisies,
tending the garden of another
Transient in Transition.

I wait, I wait, and I wait,
head hung,
floppy-eared and puppy-like,
for your sun to rise on me—
for Me to rise like the sun.

HAPPY NEW YEAR

Angel wings arranged.
Couture gown of ivory satin,
luxurious and sprawling,
silky tides
trickle and toe a silver lake glittering.

Wink of memories—
disease-addled filmstrips
popping the projector,
champagne bubbles breaking,
tumbling upward to bleed the crystal rim—
chalice of Hollywood tears.

A starlet has fallen.
Expanse of night overhead:
Beauty of Mystery
Secured in the black—
a promise in the appearance
of nothing glancing back.

Three, two one...
her girls smell too.

Her throne a decaying thing,
salt-rubbed by coastal air—
A paltry price
for a childhood stolen,
manipulated,

left for dead in a dusty border town.
Her shadow forever wandering the desert
Seeking refuge,
Seeking oasis,
Searching for a soul.

MADAM

Mother's watching.
Hardened clay mask face—
angles and valleys—
moon-shaped feathered pout from years of hard living.

Cigarette smoke unfurls, expanding,
whispered apologies unrealized—
Atonement—
an offering to the gods,
last morsel of hope unbridled,
reaching for night's Embrace...

Faint patina of glimmer smudged,
Orion's belt,
leather worn and slung,
jutted hip sauntering the sky.
The pulse of Viejo Puerto Vallarta
seducing an aged dancer's soles.

Keeper of working women,
all exaggerated eyes and lips,
Do you want me?

Counting her cut,
every peso a reminder—
sticky nights fumbling behind cantinas—
No choice, No voice.
The stink of generic aftershave
slinking on her skin still,

The way they *smell*,
Her girls smell too.

Her throne a decaying thing,
salt-rubbed by coastal air—
A paltry price
for a childhood stolen,
manipulated,
left for dead in a dusty border town.
Her shadow forever wandering the desert
Seeking refuge,
Seeking oasis,
Searching for a soul.

HONEYMOON

It was a beautiful ceremony.
Daddy was there
tucking jasmine in my hair
and you,
perfect in a rented penguin suit,
shiny at the knees and elbows.
We clambered up the courthouse steps,
arm in arm, Bonnie and Clyde.

The sun, a sparkling beacon
beckoning us,
exchanging tin foil rings
like children in the woods.
You proposed,
circling me in sturdy arms
over Clams Casino and Bloody Marys,
celery stalks swimming in our glasses.

We searched the East River,
gulls, fish, anything living,
cackling at the thought,
making maps of our hands.
Yours running lightly over mine,
mine on yours.
Our love, deep and glowing,
magma simmering below the surface.

How I crave the imprint of your body
in our bed,

you cradling me,
nipping at my ear,
hands clumsily raking locks of my hair.

I know you're only at work
but I miss you.
Across the buildings and bodegas
bustling in Midtown
I feel,
I know
you miss me too.

LYNDA BENGLIS SERIES

After a recent visit to the new museum of contemporary art in NYC, I fell in love with Lynda Benglis' work. She is famous for her "poured paintings," sculpture and installations. As with my Cindy Sherman series, the poems I write are a mash-up of my interpretation of Benglis' work as well as a poem meant to stand outside of the work on its own. The process of writing poetry about art is called ekphrasis, *which means "out" and "speak" in Greek. It is the verbal/written description of a work of art. I practice a less literal version so that my poems are inspired, not defined by, the work.* —A. J.

PERFORMANCE

Upon viewing "Phantom Series"

Cotton balls stoppered-up
like lake-effect snow
creep on garbage heaps.
I feel your arms about my heart
when the East River breathes.
The puff of a sweater against my back—
scarf snake-like, holding a pattern,
tracing my body like a beast holding sway.

The shrill banshee wailing wind
laps the lake where I'm from,
whips it up into meringue peaks
lit with electro-plankton.
It bleeds the glowing disease
like sticky fingers printing,
embossed on me

when I moved East
to dwell in the echoes of my soul,
magically pulled out and removed like a map.
Day-glo arteries,
a lacey network of highways,
feed dangling limbs gone numb,
connected only by the gallery of disembodied voices
I've followed here.
This path, a trail of hope and fear
projected:
the Art of a perfect start.

BUPRENORPHINE

Upon viewing "Mu"

Mu receptor receiving:

Euphoria: plain wave,
a whitewash of pure pleasure
deeply glittered,
gold leaf-dipped and jeweled;

Analgesia: suppressed
opulence spread speedily to coat
the synapse's spark,
and keep protected from;

Physical Dependence:
on a warm reception
upon arrival, breezy tropics
imagined in metal tones;

Miosis: narrowing
the eye line of sight—
kaleidoscope of muted neons
shot through electric static;

Respiratory Depression:
cloud cover suffocating
slowly the snow angels
we made, age eight;

Reduced GI Motility;
inability to remember
lily of the valley as ivory bonnets
ferrying the dead;
Unknown: lights strung up
like blinking rainbows
painting the River Styx
to set our boat to sea.

LUSTRE

is the light filtered from stars,
pinholes of pilfered space dust sprinkled,
fallen through city smog
in luminous layers, and set
upon the skyline—
a glorified nuclear swamp.

WAVELENGTH

Upon viewing "Red and Blue Jungle Gym"

I am professional neon,
an intricate series of Technicolor
veins and nerves.

I used to sleep in shadows
where everything is pillow-like,
soft and shapeless as a smother.

An elemental seascape
unfurled like a bed of quartz
where scintillating crags
rose as mountain stone.

With each wave
I'm less transparent,
more coherent,
Alive to the beauty of shells
laid like tiles in the floor.

This electric place is fixed
as a buried language,
undecipherable to the dead wandering,
save for the whispering water's
lunar clues.

My camera swallows a sherbet sunset
set flush against your wall.

The text of my feelings in pictures,
wayward tracings of a celestial body,
as astral burning glow.
Blues, pinks, purples,
oranges and reds—
the color scheme of a dual nature—
I inhabit now
the wires of my heart.

GOD

Upon viewing "The Clocktower"

Your face is difficult to place
because it isn't a face,
just molecules of buzzing light—
a clumsy chemistry set reaction—
purposeful in aim.

You're subtle, not roaring,
a wall of pastel fireflies,
slack heat of Midwest summer,
when I was a child
I captured in a jar.

You come on like a fever,
arrange an installation of dirty cups,
unmade bed, silvery white glitter—
a snowdrift—
on my city floor.

You're normal as a lighthouse
perched on a stretch of nameless coast
where crustaceans command sea glass shores
and boats stop for nothing,
save a glimpse of extraordinary beauty.

I've suffered a life of scuffed knees
(the torture of bowing to alchemy)

I've found something shinier than me
And you're it.
Everyday I'll write to you—
I think they call them prayers.

BAYOU

Upon viewing "Tamos"

Through a creamy peach-tree mosquito light
Bald Cypress and Southern Live Oaks
sprout eaves of languid Spanish moss,
luscious with shimmering rat snakes, bats and jumping spiders.

The air plant caves absorb nutrients:
Capote, Faulkner, O'Connor—
all dregs of vintage lace dappling the pop ash,
buttonbush, dogwood and trumpet creeper.

The slow tide of swamp pulls
shrimplings and blue crabs in the grist,
knocking beds of cobbled oysters clinging—
mangroves weaving those Gothic tales,
Southern as the groaning saw grass,
I read, eyes flipped wide as flies'.

Behold God's array of Sweet Gum and Crape Myrtles
among sugarberry, Eastertide and pawpaw.
Mint julep hush of yesterday,
I come here often in my dreams,
haunted by the sound of souls—
listen: the exquisite symphony of decay.

LOVE

Upon viewing "Medusa"

Borne from the scathing pain of others,
they call her the Gorgon—
hair wild as peat
and eyes that always rain.
Every day she wears another porcelain face.

Her Park Avenue mausoleum,
built with bones of broken men,
Pops with carnivorous plants,
brooding Victoriana blooms,
ambling English roses
And the bleating beat of a beaten heart,

there—steady on the velvet wall,
surrounded by a quagmire of hatpins—
the Gorgon's Burmese ruby organ
sputters slow stains like trickles of Bordeaux,
so far removed from its calcified cage.

Made monstrous by her own beauty,
the Gorgon, traceling of a woman,
awaits the scintillating touch,
the forgiving embrace,
a naked love without borders,
without knowing,
of the blind doctor
here, finally, to stitch her as one,
to record her truth.

ROAR

Upon viewing "Zita"

Beneath a great Manhattan moon
the City, swathed in sterling,
imitates subway-like frisson of neurons
riding maps of metallic myelin.

The thrill of electric connection
switched spine-up,
suspecting serenely,
Something is Illuminated.

On upper Avenue A, I'm naked as a baby
beset with a woman's soft breasts,
middle, thighs and all—
stark and luminous in Florentine gold.

This bliss in my heart
exists in Mylar stars,
thrown to the upward onyx
like droves of doves set free to glitter,
to turn the night and make it bright.

The essentials of "me" orbit within reach
like a vast crinoline spinning—
lovers kept in lavender charoite,
friends and family folded in pink kunzite,
and those dark things that betrayed me,
stuck forever as insects in amber, sweet olivine.

Oh how fresh it feels to view the world,
to breathe it in and blow it out,
with eyes like a tigress and a newfound roar.

HUTONG

Upon viewing "Zanzidae"

Beijing, China's cultural jewel
of cinder and cement
where skyscrapers rise daily, daisy-like,
it's out with the old—the hutongs,
traditional towns within the city
that house the poor and curious,
concentric boxes bearing common courtyards,
communal squat toilets, communal water,
a sense of forced community.
In for chilies, in for brooms,
leaping from one highly decorated room to
another.

Family systems working full, filial piety—

cherry blossoms drift through windows like
abandoned wishes.

I sipped Dragon Well tea
in an immaculately kept hutong, late March.
A decrepit toothless woman with kind moon eyes
graciously prepared my cup.
Ordinary beads, ordinary garlands
strung with pride around the family Buddha like Christmas lights.
twinkling like soft lanterns dotting neighboring windows.
In Mandarin, the woman whispers, "They want to take
    our home."

Face unchanged save for a sudden wetness in her eyes—
    fear, pride?
Searching mine, I felt blind.
It was pride. She begged me to love her beautiful life,
to see its value and know that it was priceless,
that not even the Great Red Dragon could take it away.

ANTIBODY

Upon viewing "Sparkle Knot"

These bones mimic mine,
shot thru like an X-ray,
suffused with light—
the kind found in supermarket chains,
boutique changing rooms
and nuclear waste spills.

Silver ghosts of arthritis
inhabit knees, elbows, shoulders, wrists,
cerulean twinge of nerve haunts knuckles.
The fuchsia sting of inflammation,
searing the electric train from cranium to phalanges.
This bag of bones—all jumbled chakras.

Pain so excruciating it sparkles,
intent to be noticed, tended to,
extinguished and blanched
white as winter birch—
to mute that phosphorescence
that'll wake the neighbors,
bearing shovels and old-fashioned sleepwear.

This pain can't be buried.
You might as well kill me,
or ply me with enough morphine
'til I'm dim enough to let lie in the street
and slip, whisper-like, into dirty, downtown morning
when I'll light up the sky to greet the sun.

MUSHROOM

Upon viewing "Ghost Dance"

Wood-ears, buttons and other edibles huddle,
lurk hustler-like in the musky forest gloom,
among gnome huts and toadstools—
dish blue poisonous caps avoided by mothers,
daughters, local foxes, domestic pets—
Outside of St. Petersburg.
Mushrooms and their brethren cower numerously
to an edifice to the plucked and stewed:
Like a blown-glass hotel for upwardly mobile ants
this peculiar mushroom-like structure (inedible by nature)
flourishes in light, throws tones of gold and copper—
an aberration positively Byzantine—
in halos, where fungus fails to thrive
but indigo violets of all sizes break earth,
a perfect circle moat to surround
this most unusual feature.
Some say woodland fairies tend the small creation—
others, the Venice Muranos;
Either way, this earthly display:
The art of installation.

HAVDALAH

Upon viewing "Karen"

The scent of clover and sulphur,
match strike distinguished,
flick of the wrist—
braided beeswax candle dripping
layers thin, three colors.
Grandfather's grocery,
Nervous Breakdown.
Grandmother's Leukemia,
marred blood in the cup—
just a sip, now.
I was young, the sunset
smeared pastels in the sky.
Clouds braided like that candle,
it burned 'til darkness overcame,
my nose buried deep in spice.
Goodbye, Shabbas,
Hello sweet summer night.
Hello Nervous Breakdown,
this time me.
We stopped celebrating—
the perfume of cloves
a distant memory.

ANDREA KOWCH SERIES

I have entitled this new series A Midwestern Gothic. *The series consists of poems linked together to tell the story of a decaying, formerly aristocratic family in Michigan. This is something I have never done before so I hope you enjoy exploring it as much as I do. This series is both ekphrastic and narrative, and while the poems can stand on their own, they are meant to be read in concert. As with all my poems inspired by the artwork, they are merely influenced by the artist's work. I cannot pretend to know what Andrea feels about her work. I am using them to suit my own purposes. Her work is fantastic, so I hope you enjoy.* —A. J.

VIOLET MARSH

Upon viewing "Blackbirds are Gathering"

We were the Marshes,
shadow of an America aristocracy
long ago made broken,
inbred with disease and malaise.
I was the eldest daughter,
twenty-six last spring,
when I took refuge in sun-scorched wheat fields,
amber unfurling into fall,
strangled apple orchards neglected,
bordered by brass tufts in need of rain—
fat drops of salvation—
I bode my time.
I believe I am freedom,
the very essence,
embodied and bound in blankets found,
Though crows still follow—
a reminder of sickness—
the darkness of mind mediating murder.
Our once stately home of nightly crackling embers,
Father's stories of a burdened, festooned boyhood,
of Mother's stilted slip into
murky inkwells of madness—
my sisters—
wraithlike white paper cutouts of sand dollars
plunged and sinking in starfish-starred pools,
the fools, sucked in and out—
Mother's mercurial pull.

Somehow I survived,
separated by her hateful beetle eyes
as if by a membrane,
translucent and quivering

like the jelly scrim of placenta
Mother saved in jars marked Violet, Georgia, Nora, Maura, Louise.
My home, now windowless, decrepit,
overrun by spiders, mice, vultures and crows
after Father left,
after Georgia killed him,
baked him into five separate pies only she ate,
greedy meat dribbling down her malformed chin.
Like me, Michigan no longer cries.
If only I knew what to do, how to be.
One foot following another,
I'll grab the old dirt road,
slowly turning pavement,
follow down Chicago,
sing my country blues.

LOUISE MARSH

Upon viewing "Losing Eden"

I'm the youngest of the Marsh girls,
just sixteen,
yet plagued with an old woman's skeleton
riddled with worms and osteo-something—
a lack of minerals, mother says,
since I won't eat Georgia's pies
ever since Father and her fondness for crow.
This stool, all shoddy legs,
creaks, yet the view astounds:
Grasses ripple like a golden ocean,
leaves of seaweed, field-mouse fish—
I imagine our castle on the coast,
long acquiesced to land barons
and "nouveaux riches."
This here's the skull of Georgia's baby,
two years ago born, father unknown to some.
No hospital, nursemaid, midwife,
but oh, the beautiful, plush, healthy girl, shrouded in liquid pink,
crude whitish, cast-offs I rid her of.
Maura was to burn the placenta but Mother,
ravenous and vulture-like in curious, upturned shoulder
    pads,
drank a soup of it and the afterbirth, noisily slurping.
Father returned full of whiskey,
a casket of himself,
wouldn't look poor Georgia in the face
though she moaned and heaved,
activated dual voice chords like a possessed.

Mother, clever, sneaky,
swooped in and grabbed the child,
giggling with apple-red cheeks.

The swift hack of a kitchen blade, a sure surprise
Mother severed the head, much like a fish for frying.
With a dull needle, the one Nora used to darn Father's
    socks,
I tried to save her, dear God I TRIED!
She gushed, her neck, waterfalls of hell-beasts,
silent screams and just a baby!
If I held her to my breast, would she suckle?
I named her Rosemary,
planted a crude cross among the cow grass,
buried a headless body,
tiny squirming quagmire of a puzzle.
But I couldn't bear to part with her head.
Swirling bubbles of water boiled,
skin and bone uncleaved.
Muscles, tendon, fat, tissue,
I boiled her clean like Mother taught me,
baptized her, made her a true Christian soul.
No one else wanted her:
not Mother, not Father,
not Georgia, Violet, Maura, Nora—
she's my Rosemary,
Only mine.
My baby, my chapped breasts.
She finally suckles, and all the time—
grasps these swollen nipples that
dribble special milk.
Rosie was supposed to be mine
And she grows, she grows,
She grows just fine.

MAURA MARSH

Upon viewing "Refuge"

I am but a cipher of the manor born—
eighteen and but a nursemaid to poor Louise.
Neuroscience, a dream of mine—
the pleasure of late night study in a state lab,
vanished in an instant,
in Mother's retractable claws.
She shred my University acceptance letter with such hunger,
as if to feed the chatter enfeebling her tortured brain.
Neuroscience. Degeneration. Regeneration?
Separation of mind and body.
And so I separate mine.
My body lays here, my mind, elsewhere.
Chestnut hair, matted and mingled in late summer grass,
the old Lutheran clapboard church, shedding gray/white shingles
not unlike the gulls, so far from home,
that soar overhead like enormous pearls
sewn into the clam flesh of sky,
churning now with pockets of pending rain.
Bones clamor beneath this very soil,
devoid of any markers.
I can hear them when I press my ear to the earth.
We Marshes toil even in our deaths.
Our great hulking mausoleums hauled away,
embellished with Greek Gods and Goddesses,
lost in a bet by Grandfather Marsh—
for they stood, constructed of the finest Italian marble.
Now just skeletons, no doubt gussied-up in Sunday's best:

The style of nobility—when we were noble, if we were noble.
Surely unimpressed with their mass grave,
the piles and piles of bones toppled in, one after another,
with precise, calculated carelessness by the workers.
Was it contempt?
As if the Marshes weren't welcome, buried beyond church borders,
when Sunday in and out, we children fussed about in the front pews,
adults, preening peacocks, glanced about the room, white smiles in
    abundance.
Remove the bones of the dead and they shall rattle.
Gentle shake shake shake—it soothes me, like a baby,
much as the swooshing of a gray-tipped wing expanse of the gull,
now so close, as if they might carry me away.
Another pearl on their string!
Oh draw this ashen face to the sun,
make me whole again with your scintillating thread!
yes, to be rid of Mother, to be rid of Louise and Georgia,
to be rid of MARSH,
to see the lake, its breaking waves,
where I would spend the days
swimming, floating, splashing, sinking,
Knowing that dark blue porthole of a lake.

MOTHER MARSH (OCTAVIA)

Upon viewing "The Catch"

Evening and the bats descend,
moody onyx rainbow of vampire flutter
harbor for this cage from an old canary
I ate—the squeak of Georgia's bed,
Gideon's breath—40 proof dragon vapor.
I was a comely debutante,
valley flowers wiggled in braids
wrapped wreath-like round my head.
Dove gray kid gloves caressed narrow hands,
dainty wrists, dusty pink silk slip of a gown,
gilt pumps, all buttoned up.
the smell of Gideon's mustache wax, how handsome—
He was a drunk even then.
Dots, previously stars, in my early morning eyes
wake me like a fly hum, stalwart,
sticky ear gum I cultivate—
the better to hear the devil's sermon
I'm blessed to receive.
The Dark One lives in bats like these,
I collect at 6:38pm this time of year.
Odd of mind, medicate, rehabilitate,
Made Silent.
This brain is a miracle, perfect at keeping time.
Every two years, out came a monster.
They serve the Darkness now, the furies,
but Violet ran away,
abandoned her "sick" mother,

truth-speaker, full of fuzz-making pills.
I am a cannibal. Ate my own thumb!
Devoured that beast's placenta, afterbirth.
Dried the girls' parts in clay jars

like fish sauce in Thailand—
Savages! I'll show them the Devil,
his prowess and preference for
attack-makers.
Slippery slugs flip-flop up my ribs,
itch, can't scratch something evil,
must preserve the doom.
I must drink batshit coffee breakfasts collected daily—
guano—I spread in my hair, on my face
to mark the clan of Satan.
Maura and that damned church...
I wish her soul eternal black and coal brittle!
I'll show you eternal and buy time by the Book of the Dead.
You watch me, Gideon.
Stuff your throat with furiously beating silky bat wings,
the way you battered my Georgia
and left me to the demons
who serviced me.
They gave me pleasure, made me scream,
howl even, if only through the cotton mouth
of an old witch pumped full of Thorazine.

GEORGIA MARSH

Upon viewing "Apple of My Eye"

Those crows'n crickets'n flies
spread in my pies—
little markers of death—I've made
this same dinner since age five.
Silly bunnies, flighty dears,
my sisters only know how to live
as if they wore price tags round their necks.
They bat eyelashes,
clumped spiders thoroughly drunk
and draped languidly across their cheeks
when they sleep.
I'm awake.
I don't use my body,
though at 24, it's been taken much as Mother's,
And by the same man—
Gideon—who left us in the dark—
Mother to the demons,
and to our beautiful child,
made entirely of hope and ribbons,
gentle gems, fairy dust and feathers,
stitched together at the neck
like Frankenstein's monster
by poor, startled Louise,
little lamb to slaughter so she mews
to reverse Mother's hands.
make their motion freeze mid-air,
disappear, like I made him disappear,

in dingy clay pots and pans of my youth.
Trickle of inner demon sweat,
I feel you Mother, your hand,
gripping inside my ribcage
take what's left—a heart?
I don't hear your devil cries but I try. I try!
Mother giveth, mother taketh,
take anything you wish,
I'll live my life for you,
I'll cook you dinner every night.
and if the end comes bleaker in the night,
Mother, mommy, with an outstretched arm,
an open palm, fingers stuck up like fruity knives,
I'll grant you the very first bite.

NORA MARSH

Upon viewing "No Turning Back"

I was taught to feel of pain
a wheel-less carriage, on which fanciful tablets
of morphine sulphate rode swift and deep,
green like the beguiling fairy that jaded
Great Grandfather Marsh's golden slatted spoon,
flick of blue alcohol fire lick
her chrysoberyl gossamer wings singed.
Pain in absentia.
The memory of consumptive beauty—
Sickness glittering eyes like a child's art project,
dollop of crimson blossoming at the neck
of diaphanous white nightgowns, billowing silk.
A gallery of bloodless faces,
painted a Rossetti pallor—
the cruelty of quarantine.
And I, present day,
Consumed by nothing but stale Marsh attic air.
Violet and I shared a womb,
biology, intuition, Mother's hatred.
Numbness our punishment, limb for limb, always the same.
Greek for "shapes," morphine, made us Supernatural,
yet pliant, sand in a storm, capable of shifting our shapes.
Spirits draped discarded like dirty laundry on couches,
hanged from leaky ceilings—we communed.
Griselda, pawing kitten-like, an old lawnmower.
Great Aunt Marine held vigil over Samuel,
bloated body decomposed, rotting heirloom tomato colors—

a dim, half-soul lingering between two worlds
we knew intimately like a shared body.
I wished to sing their songs,
a soaring love of the spirit realm,
of human detritus and squandered souls
bleating as sheep to slaughter
or silent, receiving a moody sunset.
And I was tied to the barracks of the attic,
glistening cave of spider spit and dead appliances,
a sea of unopened whiskey bottles asking for Daddy.
And Violet became a black orchid,
a child of the night skulking in cat shadows—
Together, we learned Pain.
Round burrs—woodland anemones bobbing in glistening
     ponytail pools,
emerald mossy-slick stones spraining ankles (Violet's),
electricity of nerves pinched in vertebrae (Mine).
I'm coming to you, Violet,
Now a Woman Unbound.
Autumn's burning brush spreads to take this house,
I prayed every day,
and in these flames, the face of God.

WEDDING MARCH

Upon viewing "Chosen"

I was the chosen Marsh
A slip of a girl, just fifteen,
in Mother's wedding dress.
A whirling dervish I set free
in a whisper of a dream cobbled from silken lace,
a whale's spray pattern of pearls
set like ivory beluga roe in the sheer bust
budding with tight tulip breasts
that I could call my own.
Thoughts of Philip's fingers gripping slender, virgin hands—
fingers I would feel inside me, deep,
pulling me inside-out,
perfectly round, just like his instrument of knowing me.
Wet with longing, I would sigh small streams between my thighs.
The hayride bounded round and round again
under carousels of candy starlight,
hungry mouths devouring,
stuck like saltwater taffy in a marriage pact.
Memories of that country fair,
How the air knocked out,
a dervish made nervous schoolgirl stumbling,
the clanging hammer assault of "Wedding March"
and I became reed-thin and sparse as my anemic bouquet,
struck down by sudden wily wind.
And there was no Philip.
No man but Daddy, dapper Daddy—
his shoes auras of light in the mist.

I would make him my own.
I take you, Daddy, to be mine,
to have and to hold,
for better or for worse,
for richer or for poorer,
in sickness and in health,
to love and to cherish;
from this day forward until death do us part.

COOKING LESSONS

Upon viewing "The Visitors"

Even though I'm seven,
they still call me Baby Louise—
including Nanny Beulah,
whose skin recalls the color of chocolate icing,
and feels just as smooth
(daydreaming about my kitten tongue lapping it up).
Crystals hang from her ears and twinkle, bump together,
lull me to sleep with their charm—
I think she's got magic in her
and I think Mother's afraid.
Even though they don't want me
(I know so 'cause they shout "leave us alone Baby Louise!")
I come and cook with wild-eyed, slender Georgia,
Maura, pimply now and eyes glazed over like a proper doughnut,
like when she reads books, which is most of the time.
I make blueberry pie filling stick to my nose,
Georgia's hand, Maura's arm and they cry "Shoo!"
It's always the same when Beulah leaves for the store.
Georgia's in the kitchen dragging Maura and her book,
Violet and Nora holed up like rabbits making more rabbits,
and Baby Louise tugs at Mother's dress pending silence.
The only thing that shocks me so,
I've noticed it from time to time,
is Georgia's serenity while she bakes:
her deftness with a knife.

SYNTHETIC STARS

Upon viewing "Night Hill"

I came for stars but there were none.
Daddy let loose the ropes that bound me,
Mother heavy in a Seconal sleep,
and the sky was pregnant with rain,
yet starless.
An old carriage turned on its side,
bone dry, perfect kindling
to keep my kin at a distance,
lay in the field just a frog-leap away.
Us Marshes, always airing our dirty laundry,
our panties and stockings in public,
for the world to see.
Strike of a match.
The ashes soar on wings of orange glow,
shooting stars alight in the bright!
A fertile fire ravaging,
catching dead grass near by.
I have made stars from destruction
constructed from pure light!
Drowsy, tired now,
collapsed on the grass,
I think of what Violet and her hair,
flaming red,
would look like,
littered with ashy stars—
small spring blooms,
lily of the valley bonnets

or the beginnings of cherry blossoms
from an old rickety carriage—
now more ash than wood.
How we can make stars,
how we can make fire
so effortlessly,
how it splashes across the plains late summer
without a match strike,
leaving hellish pools.
That truly is a miracle, if miracles exist.
I believe they do.
Something to do with ghosts—
and I know many—
though I do wish they'd stop borrowing my clothes.

VIOLET AND NORA DIG FOR CLAMS, AGE 10

Upon viewing "Marsh Hare"

Festooned in "proper" clothes Mother laid,
those patchwork lacey tiers of doom,
Nora and I,
frogged about in the farthest, nastiest pond,
beyond the misery of watchful eyes of the mansion.

Downhill from the boat shack
where lonely remnants of oars,
half a canoe,
a martini shaker and cracked set of glasses
huddle by a hacksaw,
rusty with pond dew and lack of use
all wade:
somewhere between life and death.
They ache to be found,
to be noticed,
to be carried to the decadence of what was our mansion—
or at least the barn.

The "thwwap" of my wellies for the dirtiest pond,
when Nora, jumped right in,
a leech growing fat on her biggest toe.

Our little pond,
fond of mutant plankton,
and frogs of red tincture,

surely ought produce a clam of some sort,
like our Great Lake, where we were forbidden to swim?

Oh, to feel the lip of its rough-hewn tiger shell!
Both our short arms scuttled 'round the murky sand,
as we swallowed brown buggy water,
tossing pond creatures at one another,
wrapped in ribbon necklaces of weeds.
Then, silence.
A tiny malformed crustacean-like orb!
Nora jimmied the bulging little thing open.
We nudged it awake, eyes wide as Georgia's pies.

Mouths agape, silent screams escapes in droves.
A beating heart, liver, spleen, gallbladder tangled together,
and one milky, rheumy eye off-center
watched us lazily, but watched nonetheless.
Lumps of cold blue, sick-making green,
bruised purplish-mercury red-blackish—
Our Proud Clam.
A freak.
A Marsh.

Even our land,
vast and sweeping through it was,
bred sickness, contained poison,
was made evil.

It was then I knew Nora and I would escape.
Unaware though she was
and away with the spirits,
I learned to keep mine close at a young age
for times like this.

And we would take the clam,
alive or dead.

WOLFGANG TILLMANS SERIES

As a poet, I seem to come back to the ekphrastic model time and again. Something draws me to the collaboration between art and poem, and the poem my reaction to a work of art produces. Cindy Sherman, Lynda Benglis and Andrea Kowch have been previous inspirations for me, along with cultural and literary idols, and now I explore the abstract work of German photographer Wolfgang Tillmans, the first male on whom I have done a series. On the heels of the publication of Abstract Pictures, *Tillmans' spellbinding book encapsulating his abstract work, I'm diving in.*

According to Tillmans, his Abstract Pictures *are "photographs made without a camera, purely with light...they evoke all sorts of associations like skin, or astronomy, or chemicals dissolving, and it's all done by the brain." Some of the photos appear to have been photographs that "suffered" in the developing process while others, as Tillmans says, appear as blips of pigment, light, skin, etc.*

I envision this series to be challenging, yet simultaneously rewarding. I hope you'll find it to be the same. —A. J.

PSALM

Upon viewing "Quarry 2001"

Quarries.

Limestone, gypsum,
marble, granite...

All inverted skyscrapers
glimmering,

converted swimming
holes placid and clear,

dreamcatchers catching

the prayers of the dead.

My quarry is a threadbare
wood

of scatter-patterned trees
where Rorschach leaves
bleed red ink in spooling pools.
I scrawl my prayers on sun-bleached rocks
from which I and other common ghouls
spin tales of strange journeys
captured in the eaves of the book

The rumblings of the noble dead
inspire melodies of the living,
and watercolor woods sing the song: freedom.
Eyes shut like ancient scrolls
to the metallic clanging of Manhattan—
anxieties of light scintillating night—
undulating rhythm, striving heights:
My quarry, in photonegative form.

Sing for the blind tentacles of faith,
a higher power roving an unlikely wood,
if only for everyday miracles
when all feels hopeless,
rough-edged and sharp in the dark.

My quarry is the picture of love—
hidden in a city bustling with lost souls.
It's a still place where constellations of star bodies
fall about as confetti in a cobalt sky,
illumine a blessed earth of anomalies
like the improbable quarry river
swimming towards Chicago
so I'll always know the way home.

We're all anomalies
reclaimed.
We celebrate them every day.
Amen

THIRD COAST

Upon viewing "Freischwimmer 151"

is third coast best coast?
Lake Michigan—
swath of temperate
cobalt, fouled up
by summer waves,
(tranquil trimmings),
or winter—
when steely plates jigger—
(muskellunge and
northern pike
schooling)
a mechanism
of jaws.
the beaches cleave
Chicago,
city of
Clandestine Phosphorescence,
like
freshwater clams
cluttered up,
shells clamped
to ears that are mine:
another punk
playing Dirty Harry,
paging Debbie Harry
out to
save the world

in a rowboat,
a leopard coat,
and two rings on
each hand.

DREAM ESCAPE

Upon viewing "Strings of Life"

Is how I imagine
Iceland,
buried in a snow
the colors of opals,
where a cutting burgundy sphere,
neither sun
nor moon
warms icicles in hand
until they splinter—
become fragmented.

These northern lagoons
harbor
deep-sea jellies,
shrimp and anglers—
strange pursuants of a state called
"flux."
they speak in watery runes,
neon blips that
throw electric pulses
to me,
testing invisibility
in a thermal spring
of hospital heroin,
(where neural dendrites bathe
in second-stage sleep)

building a language
to stave off death.

In this nightless place
where the funeral march
is but an echo:
a call to scrawl
the stories of the living,
awake or sleeping.

WELCOMING THE TROOPS

Upon viewing "Blushes #28"

Powdered pigment
sold to makeup pros
reminds me of Grace Jones,
her slick of orange lips
and fuchsia brow
slouching toward lavender.
Those thumb sweeps of war paint,
pulsing plunge of aortal heat—
her smooth, iron-throat call to dance,
a song for all soldiers:
march full fury to the beat.

ROAD TRIP

Upon viewing "Time, Action and Fear"

I trace barefoot loops
like quarter moons waxing—
people prints—
on the blond wood
of my apartment floor.

Today I've let the wind in.
Though winter's newly hatched,
the city's soft like Santa Fe,
a land of peach, moss, adobe red
looms low on the horizon.

I wear a cashmere blanket
like some kind of broken uniform,
and await the setting sun,
while a prism goblet sends
strange rainbows,
searching for its wine.

And so I pass the time
singing songs of the Southwest
and the desert's earthen hues,
where winter's but a whisper,
and souls don't need their shoes.

MILLAIS PAINTS OPHELIA

Upon viewing "Neutral Density"

Ophelia, we remember you
resting stiffly on your back.
The young and bloodless
mad girl drowned,
face above a reedy bath.

To drown oneself in such a
river

where lilies clear the surface
glass,

you'd have to lie down on
your stomach

and hook your head below
to watch the life in all the river
trail your fishy woman scent.

The flowers scattered through your hair
you planned to wear, a virgin bride.
They wove them in a chain of rope
to drag the river, flip you over,
smooth your gown.

PATTI SMITH SERIES

Straight on the heels of the completion of my Wolfgang Till-mans series, which flew by as if I were possessed, I'm ready to tackle my next series, inspired by images culled from Patti Smith's Camera Solo, *her first American museum exhibition to focus on her photography, which debuted at the Wadsworth Atheneum Museum of Art in Hartford, CT.*

By now, it's obvious I like to work in the ekphrastic form, which ranges from poems that literally interpret a work of art to what I like to do, which is more of a free association. I capture the feelings the image or work evokes in me and set out to write a poem completely independent of the work of art, yet which could also be read right alongside the image.

This next series will be completely different from anything I have ever done. I've never had any kind of relationship with the artists I "collaborate" with. And while I've not yet met Ms. Smith, I have always felt a deep connection with her, as if our souls rubbed up against one another at some point. Yes, each poem will have a corresponding image, but my study of Smith goes deeper. I am an avid fan of her music and listen to it often. I also read all of her poetry and writings. It was not until after I finished Woolgathering, *however, that I knew this project would be the most difficult for me. I am so enamored of her writing style, her diction and syntax, that I must be careful not to slip into her style and lose my own voice.*

The photos appear simple but are imbued with Patti's eye for iconography and personal history, as well as mine, since she is an inexplicable part of my life. The poems I began in the Tillmans series and onward reflect a self-study that wouldn't have happened without my urge to write a collection of poems based on everything Patti and her work mean for me. I am coming into my own as a poet and I owe it in great part to a certain punk poet, who inhabits the city but has the soul of a country girl. Her voice, her writings, and now what she wishes us to see with her eye, bring me closer to who Patti Smith really is, and how we're alike and how we are distinct.

I have nothing but admiration for her work, and while I admit a bit of hero worship is at play, this series is primarily a self-study, as mentioned before. What can I learn from the revolutionary woman and what does it mean? I couldn't be happier to start 2012 off with this experiment.

Happy New Year and may this year be better than the last.
—A. J. 12/31/11

MEMORIES OF FENDERS AND OTHER GUITARS—BUT ESPECIALLY FENDERS

Upon viewing "Fender Duo-Sonic"

"The scene is the same,
and though I try to imagine
plinking starry guitars,

and while I spend my
Time listening to a foreign
contralto sing the truth,

the earth is everywhere."

—Frank O'Hara, "February"

I could feel reverb like summer bugs,
rocking in a jar—no exit—
no, not today, nothing
but the lightning pulse,
the rolling of their bodies inside the glass,
flailing about electrically like
the girl in navy cords,
the lines not so close to each other,
not so far, dancing, *dancing*,
in a white magically shrinking shirt signed by Ultimate Fakebook.
She was smoking holy cigarettes
under the majestic lights of The Fireside—
the smoke, penance for a punk promise
she made to Joey, Lou, Leonard, Patti, Debbie and David—
to be important, have her own show.

If only I could still make it in New York,
with a moleskine and a Bic pen, like I heard,
if I could make it to the Bowery, revel among our living heroes
and those gossamer ghosts full of my hope like balloons
that hover above the land of the down and happily outsider.
Mars Bar just closed,
The fire escapes around our window start a game of Chutes and
    Ladders
so, so far out of reach even I couldn't play.

If I could touch his guitar,
strum its broken baby-bird metallic strings
barefoot in the living room like it's mine,
and smell his dirty man chypre;
I'd bottle the moment in a porcelain flask
crafted somewhere in Sweden, Germany or was it Denmark?
I would. I would. I would.

Now I'm a woman living in a burn unit
clutching to my fluids on poles,
waiting for a visit
from the man whose fingers find my spine,
though it's hard because I'm not skinny,
but I'm "so damn beautiful" he said,
and some other people say so too.
To him, my ribs were strings
some bunches—chords—
swinging softly from fret to fret:
He played me minor like how I should sound.

I thought of the Fender and my beat-up boots
and I saw Dee Dee Ramone
who played something like that on the bass,
paradise of simplicity,

where you'd love to discover a melody,
But it's a bit religious when I'm struck,
loveless by a dame in a kid-glove,
guitar sound a plotted story, grouping of notes,
that makes my heart sing ferociously,
and shakes a quiet riot in my soul.
I know that's what they mean by living
every day with your *whole*.

FOR A DANDY

Upon viewing "Robert Mapplethorpe Chelsea Hotel"

You had such beautiful hands.
Oscar Wilde fingers

every knuckle
beringed

with irregular
treasures.

Sometimes I think
you were astral
projected,

some aural thing up
North

come down to play.

And the rhythm's in the roll, you'd like to say,

and the rhythm's in the roll.

You showed me yours so
I showed you my Bataille.
The smell of vintage paper,
eyes dilate,
ink within,

The Story of the Eye
pressed in your back pocket
like a prayer book for a dirty kid.

A voice slender as your hips
passed, like your cigarette smoke—
a whistle trough thin lips
when we kissed:
the force of your life, or something like it,
drawing me in—
the thin skin of our sweaty sins—
Oh God, I fell for you.

And so we began the binding of books,
sewing spines with leather scrap,
as Mary made lace—
trans-Atlantic snowflakes coded with
messages crafted
by the wisdom of aging hands.
A ring rested like a secret
in the folds of her wedding finger.
Mary made lace with her hands.

When you and I bound books
we rocked and we rolled—
we rocked and rolled
when we bound books
And the rhythm's still in the roll I suppose
when our spines meet
as we lay our bodies down
for someone like God to keep.
In the morning you'll be a vapor,
save for 2 Nat Shermans arranged
like train tracks on my desk,

always going the same way,
never meeting for a longer stay.
I'll smoke and greet the later dawn,
buds of blood from needle pricks
slickening my fingers.

I KNEW A DRIFTER, I WAS ONE TOO

Upon viewing "Arthur Rimbaud's Utensils"

"Hit me up baby and knock me down
Drop what you're doing and come around
We can hold hands 'til the sun goes down"
—Nick Cave & the Bad Seeds, "Babe, I'm on Fire"

I watch you eat your morning eggs
somewhere on Ludlow
at three in the afternoon,
neat as a accountant
counting toast.

Last night I let in your leathers
and whiskey smile.
You kissed my mouth,
blessed this whirling dervish mind.
"No sleep for the dead,"
either you or I said.

And for all the aching in New York
I bit your thigh,
it tasted just fine.
We got sweaty,
stealing love from one another
like sixteen year-olds
in the back of a Chevy.

And it felt *right*
to collaborate,

with a kindred soul—
something in the spill,
so good, so good, so good.
we prayed again, right to
Nick Cave's plaintive wail,
passing stories of the human spirit
in poems, songs,
and the silence in which greatness lives.

For we are great,
we'll be okay.
When you're bred in rock'n roll
and a similar badness
you survive—
monsters of camouflage,
archers spot-on in the dark—
partners in crime packing heat.

We're getting older,
Sleepyhead,
so say the soles of our feet.
We'll dance through dusty towns,
barefoot,
boots strapped to our backs.
And when we're too alone
to hold hands,
I suppose you'll write the music,
and I'll write the words.

You're a bad boy, Rimbaud,
But baby, so am I.

NARCOTICA

Upon viewing "Cherub Fountain, San Servino"

I am a cherub
in post-punk regalia,
I wear a neo-Edwardian poet suit
with nuts and bolts for a tie.
My lace mantilla,
a velvet burned-out curtain,
Babel, Babel, Babel, Babel,
I begin to say.

I'm laid like a piano
out on my bed,
one key stretched after another –
black, white, black, white, black—
sharp on tacks, flat back,
I'd like to be played today.
A Rachmaninoff please,
my eyelashes are heavy
from sifting out the breeze
that mills about like dragon bees—
the Rachmaninoff, please.

Babel, Babel, Babel, Babel,
today there is no pain.
Take me for a walk before I swim—
my brain is soaking with the dishes
and old New York.
Cy Twombly's done my portrait
in an intra-dimensional calligraphy.

Does art look and feel the same
on the other side?

Sister Faithfull,
Sister Smith,
are we to share our heads?
Will you catch my cherub ringlets
falling down my back?
Patti, I will keep your braids
hidden in my drawer,
Babel, Babel, Babel, Babel,
turn your wheel that turns the world.
I am your apprentice,
shaking at my little wheel—
it turns the pages of my story,
spins them evenly like wool—
soft in the telling,
swift in the pull.

Hello God, do you believe in me?
Blink once for yes,
two for no,
I've only got my words to give.
They come out like confetti
falling.
I search in footprints,
earthen beds where shadows sleep,
and pray my prayers
in your many marking books—
Babel, Babel, Babel, Babel,
is all I know to say.
For we are monks and lonely punks
set in lazy chains,
singing of our fuzzy plight
in Babel-oh-knee-uh.

WRITTEN IN A TAXI FROM FIRST AND FIRST TO 79TH AND WEST END

Upon viewing "Graland Moscow"

In the morning I am infant blind,
reaching about in the sheets
for my book of prayers
written on gauze; soft, thin,
holes small enough to hide an electric rose.

When every day is a year,
use the smell of rose intensified
to smudge the corridors,
the frequent shifts,
plunges,
nocturnal lifts
of the brain that I own—
theme park of rides—
that bobs like a buoy in a harbor,
lights swinging
in my downstairs neighbor's tea garden.

I'm no Plath,
no Woolf or Sexton,
I only know how to die the common way.
If Jews could bleed stigmata-like,
I'd trail my martyr blood
over linoleum kitchen tiles,
down the broken stairs,
out the garbage door:
RODENT STATION,
and on my happy street

to feed trees
still interested in weathering the chill.

Those moons are scars—
I've washed the blood away,
all of it, away.
except where it might be loved
as rubies glinting—melting? in the sun.
I've made a pact to play the course
and that is why I stay.

I scan my soul for something smart,
a message, tucked like a secret,
behind an aching heart:
Bless this child that fears the sleep,
Bless this child that feels so deep—
And so I wear a daisy crown,
to keep this child, make her grown.

THE IMPOTENT WING REVISED (FOR ODILON REDON)

Upon viewing "Christoph Schlingensief, Munich"

She's a winged beast inside-out
with a headdress of bandages,
each a wraithlike loop
stained in spots with ink,
sticky as blood,
where it can't absorb the air.

She carries a kitten lion like a
locket

in the furrow of a rib—

outside defender, attorney of
heart—

only she can decipher his primal
mews.

The smell of antiseptic,
strong like ether,
swishes like gin in a glass.
Drink up, pretty beast!
Let's make you all better.
Aren't you tired of knocking about
hospital rooms?
Like a monk of antiquity,

she writes it as it was,
the story of a winged beast inside-out,
organs and bones, a mini museum,
all-access, all-see,
with a kitten selling tickets
and a tiger standing guard.

I found her exquisite.
All those bones and organs
packed perfectly like grapefruit in a crate
from some sunny place
where the alligators sleep.

If I could creep into her room,
read her book,
notice that it was mine—
I'd take it and let sleeping kittens lie.
I'd notice she plays records like Television,
Tom Verlaine whining something lovely
with all the curtains drawn.

In all a record's revolutions,
some kind of evolution coming,
I can feel it visible in my bones.
The essence of structure blooming—
slushing 'round in newly fallen snow.
It fell while we were sleeping.

A SCRIBBLING PRAYER

Upon viewing "The River Ouse, East Sussex England"

I am Morpheus and you
are my lover

if only a night, I tug at
your dreams,

ribbons of veins, map of
transit,

rest your mind as you
rest mine,

for it's been a long trip
to meet you.

Your fingers leave prints
on me,

and glow from my lungs,
the exhale a plumage of smoke so thin
it seemed a cloud I brought from the sky.
And when we spend the night,
I'm a ghost falling through you,
catch in the back of my throat,
thunderclap of brain honey dripping,
I tuck a poppy behind your ear.

Catch you in my trap.
ephemeral thing,
languish in the depths—
a projection of stars
are really the lights of the city...

...stream of consciousness,
let me take you with me.
I'll carry you on the lilting winds
of a tumbled heart,
beating, bloody, ticking thing
pleasantly slowed—
a Canadian flush across the plains.

But in your sailboat you will row,
to see the sparkly things,
yet I am radiant,
the right kind of shiny—
you belong, an offering,
glittering my arms.
We're two hearts connected by string.

For wherever you go,
you'll find me.
rustling in the thick of the reeds,
folded like a swan in wait
garnishing your bed.
Might we be the better for it?
'Cause I love you,
body and brain—
that's all I could possibly say.

THIS IS NOT MY CITY, PART 2

Upon viewing "Self-Portrait, NYC"

Patti, I let a man inside
who you let, one time,
inside of you.
I sought transference,
your transparent webs
to bungle through,
to find you,
lily of the valley
bathed in shade,
the tinkling of your bells,
your presence—
a skittering of Zen koans.

You compose elegies on graph paper,
boxes bordering slanted script so sacred,
and I, requiems in a lavender moleskine
with no boxes to exist outside of.
I have this body to journey with,
I seek a sojourn of the soul
in a city that has failed me,
a New York that comforts and repels
at once.
Mixed vial of glitter and dirt,
the city glows dimly
under a patina of stifled dreams
suppressed under the weight
of NEW MANHATTAN,
playground for a populous

of soul-sullied rich kids
demanding their feed.

Though I am a solitary in nature,
I'd like to walk the way of the Buddha,
of God,
in a dirty venue
where punk rock breathed its first breath.
You peeled off your shirt,
baring your breasts to the world.
You sang of Pollock, of Hendrix,
of Rimbaud and Baudelaire,
of Babylon—
all lovers trapped in your elevator shaft.
They exploded through you
as they do me—
your ribcage,
shrapnel in a rapturous blast,
heavenly and blinding.

Tuck my scraps in your packet of jewels,
scattered ruby beauties.
I'm pressed in your pocket deeply
when for so long
I orbited obliteration,
dizzy as a whirling dervish.

Let me kiss your third eye,
bless it the best I can
to strengthen my gait,
vein-like ropes a tether
to your soul.

I seek transcendence

and Patti, you transcend.
Here Robert, here Fred,
here soldiers of my heart light—
a good man is hard to find.

Patron saint of poetry,
direct line to the angels,
please hold my hand—
I'm primed this time.
From the slow undulations
of Atlantic waves,
you'll pull me through
to that city on the Lake,
sinking into life
and whatever it holds.

REFLECTING ON THE
PATTI SMITH SERIES

As I stated before I began my Patti Smith series, the poems in the series were meant to be a searching of the soul. Some were incredibly painful to write and many explore spirituality, right along with sexuality, which are topics I don't usually discuss. Patti Smith inspires me more than any other artist. Through her poetry, music and visual art, she helps me to go to that place where I often avoid.

At the start of my serious poetry career, my poems were disjointed and made little sense to many readers. At the time I was suffering from serious addiction and my chapbook, "Atypical Love Letters," published in October 2009 (the month I began to conquer my addiction) is a testament to my warped state of mind. Save for a handful of poems, I don't really connect with the writing in the chapbook.

As I got well, I didn't write for a whole year. I thought my inspiration had vanished and was somehow linked to the drugs, that I would never write a single word again. Slowly I eased myself back in to writing with my Cindy Sherman series. While I struggled to find footing, I discovered a change in my poetry, often noted by others. It made sense for one. My metaphors weren't mixed and I didn't feel I had to end every poem with some sort of lesson, like a fable. My last stanzas had previously felt disconnected from their poems.

I began to study old favorites like Marianne Moore and James Merrill and started to appreciate the sophistication of their poetry. Frank O'Hara, another favorite, opened my eyes to fun again. For once, not everything was so serious, a quality I often despise in contemporary poetry. I appreciate elegies and poems that deal with the everyday and sometimes extraordinary pain of writing because that is a part of life. But when I really dove into the poetry of Patti Smith and later,

Traci Brimhall and David Trinidad, I began to find my true voice that had been stifled by years of abuse, in every sense of the word (not from my family—they are wonderful!).

Patti opened my soul to kindness towards myself and a burning desire to write my story and to discover my whole. I am sad the Patti series is over but I believe her legacy has left a hefty mark on my soul. Where I used to struggle to write, I can't help it now—it just flows out of me every day. I feel, finally, like a poet. Poets and writers are often asked why they write and the simple answer is "because I have to. I can't not write." This is my vocation, no matter what job I hold in the real world, I will always, first and foremost, be a poet.

Thank you, Patti, wherever you are, for teaching me to transcend darkness, disappointment, fear and pain. You are fearless, and I am in your debt. —A.J.

ODILON REDON SERIES

As I began work on the Rinko Kawauchi series, I had this gnawing feeling in my stomach. Quite simply, I wasn't ready to move on from what the Patti Smith series granted me: An exploration of the soul, life, journeys and, of course, the artist as transcendent—a person rising above the chaos, a master of shape-shifting and yet, an artist as entirely authentic unto herself. When I finished the series, I felt I hadn't enough time. I wasn't ready to leave yet.

So I have decided to embark on a miniseries—only four poems—based on the graphic works of Odilon Redon, a French artist whose works are often considered a precursor to Surrealism. I have been a fan of Redon's work for years and was not surprised to learn that Smith is also a fan. Redon was one of the first illustrators to tackle the stories and poems of Edgar Allan Poe—another one of my favorites.

Redon's work runs from the heavenly to the macabre—the perfect mix for an artist like me. I hope to expand upon and continue to grow from where I ended the Patti Smith series.

And so before I embark upon the electric wonderland that is Rinko Kawauchi, I'll be working on this small series inspired by Odilon Redon. I hope you find his work as inspiring as I do (and that my poems are okay, too).—A.J.

A SIMPLE SONG FOR THOSE WE LOST

Upon viewing "A Mask Sounds the Funeral Knell"

I regret I never saw your face

when you
buried me
in potting
soil,

pushed
under like a
tulip bulb,

praying for
the kiss of
spring.

Dirt in my
mouth,

muffled
scream,

caked in half moons—

my fingernails

dug me out of that shallow grave.

Your bullet tears burrowed,

like arterial spray,
my span of back,
a Lite Brite,
rainbow of pegs plunged thru
thick of muscle, bulge of bones.

You done me wrong,
You done me wrong.
You done me undone—
with your word, your song,
transmuted thru mute lips
of your pallid mask—
I never even saw your face.

In an undercover world,
I make authenticity,
defend it to the death—
I seize that first possibility.

Among restless, replica robots
I walk my way in grace,
seal it in books stapled to stars
for all God's monsters
like you, to gaze.
You wronged me—done—
you sounded bells,
a funeral knell,
an empty grave.

I'm still alive,
another gorgeous day—

you done me wrong,
the worst kind of way.

I'll make my Art,
I will create,
stronger still,
I'll write the dark.
ART IS REAL, ART IS LIGHT,
I don't need your lies to heal.

What about you?
What do you feel?
Master of half-life,
wearer of masks—
you couldn't look me in the eye.
Before you left me
good as dead,
I never saw your face.

FIRST RAPE

Upon viewing "And The Eyes Without Heads Were Floating Like Mollusks"

There were two of them,
laughing,
scent of ether on their gloves
wrapped my brain with wild cotton,
fleecy tufts riding the wind.
One two, one two,
knocked my stuffing out in plumes,
in out, out in,
what goes up must come...

In the dusty light of dawn
I fell awake, pink skies,
discarded in an ivory Buick
whirled and banged around.
Mascara dragged a Picasso face
in sloppy lines, shaken—
a rear-view mirror clown.

Crack of rib, twisted arm,
my eyes were opals smashed.
Flicker wiggle of darting spots
like those left looming
from staring at the shock of sun.

Hush the sound, a heart stepping lightly,
hush the wound, a memory shut down,

distant as the taste of snow
on Huangshan mountain
ringed with crowns—
antique, holy, strong.

I traded poems for prayers of peace,
and combed the caves for Buddhist nuns—
all errant pearls like me,
rescued by the scoop of palm—
a life of meditation aloft,
carried in clouds of calm.

I was projected,
Body worn and weary
protected
by hummingbirds with nectar mouths,
a quest for justice never come.
I shut my eyes, passed the time
eluding fate, I moved on.

Rape is rape,
a four-letter word
I've transformed.
Rape is rape,
nothing but a word,
like love, like hate,
nothing but a word.

A THOUGHT IN FEBRUARY

Upon viewing "There Was Perhaps A First Vision"

I work so hard
to show a world

of Post-Warholian
artlessness,

all I could do,

all I could become.

bundled in my mother's
mink,

pockets packed with velvet
squares.

We're the generation
they call "entitled,"
bereft of meaning,
chasing dreams, the high,
the scream.

I reject techno-logic—
to exist is not enough.
The bold create, affect, engage
a language loved in many ways.
subject, somehow,

to growth, to change.

I've lived the lives of many passed,
Tibet's Green Goddess,
Joan of Arc,
band mate on the Bowery,
a simple serf.

I crawl the earth
for useful scraps
like silver-pointed stars,
now pressed,
into a wash of evening sky
invented just for me,
or so it seems,
intended for us poets—
still relevant,
dancing in the glow.

Electric nerves
demand meaning,
demand a hope—
a voice abandoned,
a song hummed
through the lips
of those transcended—
those transformed.

AN ENDING

Upon viewing "Profile of Light"

My bones are heavy,
lonely and winter-dry.
Fleshless and scattered like timber,
my spine is laid like a river
yet cupped in the palms
of an I Ching diviner—
moon-blue and transparent.

The snap of ribcage
sings a bundle of twigs stepped upon.
The percussion of a heart moved apart.
I knew it was coming,
like a sparrow
now dropped at sea—
buried by the ancient lunar tide—
my only place of peace.
A silent prayer
muscles through lungs and brain,
mute anger slung on lips.
The weeds in which I roll
run deep,
are tethered to the earth
by sinewy skin ropes.
The world is a place of veils
through which everything seems right

and all is good and light.
My head is full of cotton,
yet still I can hear
the grunt of a gun
and the bullet that shot you dead.

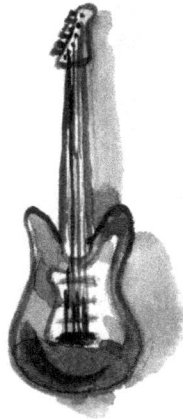

RINKO KAWAUCHI SERIES

I discovered Rinko Kawauchi's new book, Illuminance, *at the Strand, NYC's best bookstore, on E 12th Street and Broadway. I knew nothing about her or her work but the cover of her tome drew me in. It looks like an electric rose bathed in neon. I flipped through the copy that wasn't shrink-wrapped and fell immediately in love with all the color, glow and haunting beauty of her photographs. Together they are a gorgeous dreamscape. All the photographs are untitled. Below I am excerpting text from Yumo Goto's review on the* Time Lightbox *site, because I think Yumi sums it up best—why I am so in love with Kawauchi's work and how it lends itself perfectly to poetry.*

Contemporary Japanese photographer Rinko Kawauchi creates an imaginary space where the fantastical is possible—evoking ideas of dreams, memory and temporality. The images in her book, *Illuminance*, span 15 years of work, both commissioned and personal projects, and have the ability to make the mundane extraordinary, leaving poetry in the viewer's mind. This is even more apparent after the recent natural disaster in her homeland.

In her photos we see an iridescent diamond; a radiant blue sky; an elderly woman making onigiri; an infant suckling on her mother's breast. At first glance, her photographs seem simple. But her talent lies in the way she is able to evoke the primal in all of us; a depth of raw human emotion. "It's not enough that the photograph is beautiful," says Kawauchi, "if it doesn't move my heart, it won't move anyone else's heart."

I couldn't have said it any better. —A. J.

THE SOUND OF A HEART BREAKING

The sound of a heart breaking
rides on the wings of a sparrow,
smells subtle as rosewater,
and mimics the wishbone's snap
like a fist of sticks scattered
and strewn about as veins,
through which pain and sleep slink,
indistinguishable from one another.
I've been here before.
Perhaps I'll dream of horses
wild in mossy spring,
trotting the valley between rib and hip—
a sickle of translucence
flush against petal breasts.
Yes, I've been here before
but not like this.
You called me a friend so precious!
The pain of knowing otherwise
chokes,
makes broken anything we ever had.

EMERALDS

Emeralds are the peacocks of gems
buried in rings,
set in the earrings I wear
while traveling the chasms
of a mind non-linear,
the clucking sound of watches set
and the lunar glow of Tara.

The emerald belongs to woman,
to those who entertain color as opals
like O'Keefe, and Marianne Moore,
Dorothy Parker and Colette,
Anaïs Nin and Djuna Barnes.

The emerald smells
that scentless smell
of black orchids unfolding—
vaginal stars abloom
in the lotus of a palm.
Whether translucent
or deep as a Mediterranean shore,
the stone marks unconditional love,
the breaking and building of a true woman—
her written expression
on the wave of emerald breath.

FOR SID, MY CAT AND KEEPER

My cat shoulders the sea
that sluices through the cuts of me
when I'm to pieces
and the seeping black
fringe of non-human depravity
rustles/upturns my heart,
its steady beating returned
by the sure weight of his paw on
breast.

He sponges it away
with eyes wise and round as quarters,
harnesses the strength of our being
so I can walk upright,
and exacts punishment on pretend mice
so I might stopper up the tears—
those horrors I have hidden away—
yet, today, sit as chessman on a fresh board.

And he, my fierce protector,
in search of a plaything,
topples the board,
checks the king,
and returns to his bowl
slurping up a drink.

AN EXERCISE IN INTIMACY

Anna M. I loved you once,
could feel my fingers
tap tapping collarbone.
The luster of your skin,
micro beads of glow—
I wish I lick, lick, licked
on a pitted couch,
threadbare. There
the White Sox
swept the Series,
one, two, three, four,
I wanted to slide in.
Somehow, I know
how it would go:
your muscled frame
like a man's
those angel eyes—
all Woman.
Curvy lines,
those thighs like mine,
I miss that kiss,
that basement,
that couch,
underground, 2005

SISTER MORPHINE

Patti, Marianne and I
used to get high,
with pinkling animal eyes
the color of day-old kittens.

It hugged me as a dress,
in a purring Arctic,
a white postcard paradise
of Northern Lights
and nomad trails,
a creeping silence
where lady flakes fall
deep in the belly of an old bell jar.

The lids of our eyes
drop, drop, dropping
when heart slows sloshing
and angels of ice
sleep by our toes.
Focus on the symphony of lack,
the flopping of my broad mink hat
that flits atop my nakedness
away from hungry televisions.
This is bliss, oh this is art,
the lightning bug that rules the dark.

Breathe in, breathe out,
let the Sister knock you out.

You can reach me if you try,
inhabit me from my inside.
I'm here and God I'm dreaming
that this buggy glitter smacks the ceiling
and settles home inside my bones
to bring me back
anon, alone.

UNTITLED

This body
This my being
Silk-hewn projection
Pale face
On the black Lake glass
Moon blood glittering
Anxious and thick with orange
Harvest membrane drips
This slip of lavender
From the fields of Cologne
A nighttime swimming costume
Inlaid with shark teeth
For me
this my being
To scuttle worldly waterways
Plugged-in veins
That harbor passion
Tugboats, passed-on ships
I am collected
This being
This me
Captain of the key
Slender arm of lightning
Lighting up the see.

WE TOOK A SUITCASE

On the outside
Always
Not your kind
We fill 'em up
Pop pop pop
Rimbaud, you've left your trousers
In my dressing drawer
We are illegal
Not a part of
The system
The fluff
No mistress
No secret of yours
We're our own secrets
Locked in
Hooked up
An amplifier heart
Has buttons
Pop pop pop
That pill
That needle
That habit that kills
The fluff
The system
Up up upping your throat
A fall of sorts
Out the mouth

Like silver stars or
Aliens from '60s TV
This time-travel is exceptional
Outside the mind
As we
Rimbaud
As we

MANIFESTA 1

I'm prayn naked in the temple of bones
Whispren neon psalms
To a God
Whose left me lone with Poe
The weight of his wishes
A chain mail party dress

* * * *

The Beast in White
S'beautiful
Licking the stars off a sad night
Please fill my veins
Any kinda way—
Alternating/direct current
Shake me
Hands to knees.
This beast
These tears
This me

* * * *

Corporal community
Of freak and fauna
Where I am Pan
Blinking ink creatures
To the page

God don't leave me with the lights out
I'm missing you today

* * * *

If death is a reedy bed
I am Ophelia
Slurp slurp slurped down
Cuz the deafening roar of sober sun
Gallops the back of oblivia's dark horse
Sinking me
That metal dress!
I want his head on a platter

* * * *

Lunar tide stirs belly
My sex
All the trinkets/planets catching my eye
To distract me your lovemaking?
This loneliness
A volume expanding
In hands, in head
Is artifice
In a consolation city

* * * *

I am making art
Art is making me
Despite da good doctyr
Whose anesthetic finger pulls
Feign a friend
A spike sitting thru his head—

The Virgin Mary's
The pregnant Rebeca's
The blind Ariel's blood
Trickling down from neck's nape
To cracked back

* * * *

Step on me G
And you shall lose
A thousand screaming baby deaths
The beast
The best
My electric colt
The volt of torn dress (we used pliers)
Weeping in the pines
Their needles
Listless in The Temple of Bones
My house
My cries
My strong, woman thighs
Cry-baby
Cry

JOHN CURRIN SERIES

I was just about to abandon my series' themes to try and grow as a poet. However, I can still grow as my poems are evocative of how art makes me feel—not how it may be intentioned in reality. I have decided to do a short John Currin series because I love him and have decided to focus on his paintings that feature women exclusively. This won't be a lovey-dovey embrace-your-womanhood series. I'm interested in how my words can impact his images and vice-versa.

So let's have a hand for the sexiest oil painter of the moment, John Currin. —A. J.

EMERGENT URGENCY

Upon viewing "The Veil"

These handcuffs ain't shackles
when they're tethered to you.
Your heartbeat's smell's in me too
when you play me
down THERE.
Callused tippling fingers
bend spine
I'm the neck of your guitar
changing strings, biding time.

We're staring the gun
steely in its face
like Bonnie and Clyde
we'll pull it off,
flip the switch,
knock out the teeth,
and train it on sky—
those summer sucking stars.
The fizzy pop of feather lips
belong to me.
You and me, Ian,
just do it fast and cheap.

Play me right,
sing it low and deep.

The fringy roll of your sleeves
trail sand from a dark night's dip

in Lake Michigan's lick—
it sticks.
Step into my shower
I'll rain you down,
make you clean
if you make me too.

We ain't broken,
got no disease
don't need no fixin'
tumbling in a fort of sheets.
Get it get it get it here,
You know I got a car,
shoot 'em up, sweetheart,
kill 'em down,
this ground is soft and
mutable as a gesture
in the fight of sound.

We've got a family, baby,
you and me.
When you come,
I'll come too.

This flat Midwest scat sings
a ribbon ring on my finger.
Come and wrap it 'round me,
take care of me—
we'll split the deck,
and all those feckless fiends'll
cease to be seen
cuz we've got a gun,
we've got a gun.

FOR EMILY DICKINSON

Upon viewing "The Shrouded Woman"

And in this twilight
I will come,
My thwarted spine
A strangled cry,
To meet my maker—
Watch me run!

My painted eyes,
An opal thunder,
Oh my maker,
Tender hunter,
Lay me down below the Lake.
In my spinal fluid crawl
And stack these stones atop my bones.

Let me feel the blank of death
Relieved of sound,
Relieved of breath.
Save for a symphony of blood—
A flood-rush in my ears
It sings.

With every wave
Abate the ache,
Abate the stab,
Abate the shake.

Invade my lungs,
Oh happy lake!
So I may sleep
And dream of you—
You're nobody
And I'm nobody too.

NAKED

Upon viewing "Anniversary Nude"

This right here's the book a' me
spread on the sheets
that bind 'n tie.

Read my spirit's Braille with care,
those callused finger pads are prayers.
"The major fall and the minor lift,"
Leonard, dear love, come lookit me.
Lookit my eyes,
Lookit this space,
It's holy and a gentle place
between these kissing thighs I own
a moody burnished glitter flows
and mine will come—
a Buddhist nun
aboard the River Styx.

What she say?
What she pray?
What the shape 'a me today?
An ocean's moody stumbling hews,
a purple glaze upon your face
so criminal it's hard to fake.

Color me outside the lines,
love me,
play me,

all the time
and kiss the golden book we made
of punk and poets sung—I'm saved!

Oh Patti, in your double plaits,
shake me down,
shake the filler out the crown
and give me life
without the fight—
an existence authentic.

For so am I,
for so are you,
and all we sought we came to find.

DRESSING FOR DELILAH'S, CHICAGO

The visceral slip:
A leather union
for woman warrior,
pre-historic as a lie.
Lunar tides swath me in
Black Leather,
weathering the deep displeasure
of a writhing intricate
splitting of notes.
Let her in!
Let her howl the glory din
that resuscitates,
infuriates, excavates
The woman of rock,
The woman of roll,
and how we inter-lock/the whole.
The key is weeping
sullied in its slot
where secrets make thick my skin.
It's a revelation where we've been,
a qualification of beauty mis-hatched,
an oxblood plume
bloomed among *les fleurs quotidienne*.
The doyenne of street slickness—
rank and file—
set across the naked coming
thoughts strumming in/coherent,
natural as a river bending rocks,
carving out a place and time.

MIA MAKILA SERIES

HE SAID HE WAS AN ALIEN

He said he was an alien.
She said he didn't look like one.
But he was. He'd like to find his home, he said, and would she let him in?
She'd wander naked in darkness with him.
She would bury him in her.
She would swallow him whole.
She would give birth to him,
reflect him his beauty,
his crackle authenticity—
But he wouldn't let her. He was an alien, he said, and she wasn't.
Her eyes were puddles.
His hand made circles on her back.
The pulse of her pain was glitter. It burned holes in space.
She knew his words as they slipped from his lips.
She knew them by their preferred:
movie theatre
grocery list
drink
comic book store
urban beach
shopping mall
video arcade
dental floss.
She *saw* him.
His skin became hers
She wore his eyes
She lugged his lungs
She listened:

The sound of his/her breathing: slow, sad.
Something happened to him.
Something made him not okay with himself.
He was preparing to leave—
All the while, she had been preparing to stay.
A heart shattered
She felt the clatter—
She searched their chest,
A panic scanned her face
It was glass on the floor.
It wasn't hers.
He was an alien but he hurt like a man.

TEXAS

I went to visit you
to listen to records in silence,
one we've inhabited before,
where our brains cuddle
in sonic blindness
and we never touch.

I brought my records
but your turntable broke
so we hummed sounds
rolled in their waves;
your body felt like mine—
I couldn't make out your difference.

you dissolved sonatas
while I sat on your bed,
the chug-chug of your cigarette,
your backing band.
I'm inclined toward your deep
I have no fear of getting lost
I know exactly where to step
when there's broken glass on the floor.

even when we disagree
we hold hands,
pass notes to one another
thru closed lips.
I got your taste like a stamp—
a souvenir of careful kindness

where I had been reckless.
you met me in the middle.

we cracked cans of PBR
on the way to Waco,
where nothing happens.
the roads sprawl oblivion
and we hugged them
crunching Skittles and Skor bars
we tapped our boots and sang
the Ramones
we played Disappear from New York—
a game we've played for years
we've been escaping
wondering where to hide

MAX CAPACITY

For twenty-nine years
I've lived a life
With headphones on:
In sleep, in wake,
It's only the record that will change.
When I cry
I show you glitter,
The proliferation of which
Arrests tears, presses stars
They are lights in my eyes.
I don't have feelings
Because they play too loud
When you're around
And all I ask is QUIET
So I can't care if you stick around—
I have to make a living.
I harvest pearls,
I cut the water when I swim,
Carve it with the cups of my hands,
And you watch
From a makeshift pier.
I saw you dancing, I think,
Shifting your weight in a sway—
You do it all the time
But I'll never tell you,
I'll never say.
I've seen you eat me up like pills.
You try and kill the transfer of data
Between us—

Sometimes it happens
When we're around.
Don't worry, I cancel it out.
I always cancel it out.
Because even when you're happy
I'm sick with the weight of it all
And so I go swimming
I do my work,
Sometimes, I wonder
Do you ever catch your reflection?
It moves freely on the water,
Sways in tandem with mine.
It wouldn't matter if you did
Even if you shut your eyes
I'm a working woman—
I'd never have the time.

NOCTURNE

To catapult into dream is...
are fingers of dead oak
massaging midnight psalms
and wind-whipped prayers
in a smudge of sky.

It's Christmas Eve.
Religious tourists clamor:
The stained glass candle-lit
doors of the devout.
And I, just passing by,
crackle pockmarked snow
icily under foot.

Flakes fall in moody drifts.
A sleepy littering
of scintillating ephemera descends,
celestial glitter dwindling,
like starved winter stars
stitched in a bolt of stormy silk satin,
shade of late-night slate.

In a few hours I'll awaken,
a dove-grey dawn draped in melancholy,
the shimmering nightscape,
a fractal memory captured—
static as a photograph.

DAY OF THE DEAD (FOR FRIDA KAHLO) 11.2.11

Grief is a wandering uterus.

Your body-cast, synthetic
exoskeleton

for a body metaphorically
entombed.

Paint drips placenta-like on
borrowed canvas,

Your womb conjures shadow
projections

Of children, toys, bottles—

trappings of motherhood never understood.

Self-portrait aortically connected,
Heart to heart, part by part,
liver, kidney, bladder, brain,
headscarf, opal, beaded chain—
Frida, these are all of you:

The woman with the skull in her month,
with raven braids, a serpent crown,
who walks through walls and underground,
and on this day—above the earth—
In Death: the artist lives unbound.

AFTER NEIL YOUNG

You were always right,
'Bout the Needle and the Damage Done,
'Bout the beauty of the country sun
And the country man making way
In rock 'n roll gold.

Had I waited out the hurricane
And set my sights on shore,
I wouldn't be the broken love song,
A record running revolutions—
a woman on the run.

Listen here,
The old man in my heart,
Don't cry cuz your daughter's done wrong,
She'll come around in the end.
She'll make you proud—
Proud as any son.

Let those licks rip and roar
Southern Man,
Let them shield you
From the black black gun—
I know you seen it too,
The wraiths calling out for quarters
When you haven't none.

It's the scream that won't come,
The silence a plague on the tongue
Of every artist in step with a dream

And the nightmares yet to languish
With the set of a burnt-out sun.

You've seen it all.
What follows the drown
Of a sound wave?
Can you tell me
When it comes?

FOR KURT COBAIN

There's a photo of you
in my faux leopard jacket—
of course, you hadn't known
it was mine at the time.

Plastic white sunglasses
rake tangled bangs.
Pupils pin (again and again),
from which the multitude of stars
cascade a private glitter
unchecked,

unprotected as you were,
set adrift in the crowd's cushioned arms.
Another consciousness breached!
Another dream leached
from the insides of you,

the lonely Buddhist punk
with the icicle eyes—
alternately blue and grey.

O Voice of a Generation—
keep you safe,
keep you safe the best you can.
Stay where you are,
You've earned your peace.

I will travel on

NOCTURAMA (FOR NICK CAVE)

the first time I heard this album
in Brooklyn, some eight years ago
I spent the night on the couch
with an old friend.

I recount in fuzzy hues of blue
the rumble of your thunder voice
instructing me to do
what I did at the time
my back a stretch of ivory keys
and you were playing me to sleep

I've never met a lullaby
so fervent
urgent when I needed one
your lovely darkness
transformed traffic chat
took me somewhere new

I'm struggling in another city
far from Brooklyn,
Thirteen hours drive by car
and in this city
in your image
I built a boy from body parts

the boy I made
would clang my pots
would keep me up
would wake the neighbors

a violent light
he cultivated
the kind that haunts
supermarkets
fitting rooms
and nuclear waste

I let my monster loose
unfinished
a boy without his feet
I placed you on my turntable
let you spin
and drifted into meditation--
a special kind of sleep
awake

ACKNOWLEDGMENTS

Thank you to Sharon Fiffer, an author and editor extraordinaire who brought order to our project coupled with thoughtful advice. To Erik Kraft who guided us in design, graphics and nuances of publishing. We would not have been able to complete our endeavor without the able assistance and typing abilities of Sue Cicero. Importantly to our dear friend Mark Pattis, a reformed book publisher who shepherded us through all aspects of creating these volumes. We are grateful for his wisdom regarding the intricate details of our project. To Vivian and Philip for their incredible insight. With deep appreciation to our family and friends who have provided unending support and love during our journey.

Hyde Park, Catskills (1856)
Johann Hermann Carmiencke